MOTHER MARGARET MOSTYN
DISCALCED CARMELITE

CONTENTS

LIST OF ILLUSTRATIONS

AUTHOR'S NOTE

THIS account of Mother Margaret Mostyn is based on her life published in *The Quarterly Series* (1878), edited by the Rev. H. J. Coleridge, S.J., from MSS. preserved at Carmel House, Darlington. Among them was a complete biography written by Canon Edmund Bedingfeld, who was Chaplain at Lierre and Mother Margaret's ordinary confessor for over thirty years. In contemporary records and the Canon's autograph letters his surname is written *Bedingfield*. Both forms occur, but the spelling *Bedingfeld* has been used here in order to secure uniformity with that adopted in *English Carmelites in Penal Times*.

The writer is deeply indebted to His Grace the Archbishop of Cardiff, who read and approved the revised life when it was in MS., and honoured her by writing a Foreword. Thanks for the privilege of being chosen to do this work are gratefully offered to the Reverend Mother Prioress of Carmel House, Darlington, who lent photographs, and MSS. with which the earlier life was collated, and to Reverend Mother of Lanherne, who allowed use to be made of MS. annals and other matter.

Special thanks are offered to the Right Rev. Mgr William Godfrey, Rector of the Venerable English College, Rome, for his lucid Introduction which explains the bases of the supernatural favours granted by God to souls spiritually akin to Mother Margaret Mostyn.

FEAST OF CORPUS CHRISTI,
  June 11th, 1936.

FOREWORD

WE are very pleased that the life of Mother Margaret Mostyn has been rewritten by Sister Anne of Jesus. We congratulate this good Sister on the simple but eloquent way in which she has done her work. It has indeed been an exceptional pleasure to read through the proofs of this life, and as one who belongs to the family of which Mother Margaret was so holy and distinguished a member, I beg to thank Sister Anne for all the trouble she has taken in rewriting the life of this holy soul.

Mother Margaret Mostyn, as a Carmelite nun, was a true and faithful follower of St. Teresa, and she has long been venerated by her Sisters of Carmel, especially by those whose house is situated at Darlington. Doubtless her intercession has obtained many graces for the members of that Carmel, and her example has stirred many a soul to greater fervour in the religious life.

As a member of the family of Mostyn of Talacre Mother Margaret was truly Welsh, and the Catholics of Wales look to her to intercede at the throne of God that the faith of our forefathers may come back to our land. We rejoice to think that thanks to her intercession in addition to that of other holy souls, that her home at Talacre, where doubtless as a child she used to play, has passed into the keeping of a Benedictine Community. This community will doubtless cherish the Catholic memories and traditions of Talacre and in accordance with Benedictine custom, Jesus Christ, in the Sacrament of the Blessed Eucharist, will continue to reside in their Chapel. The Talacre Chapel will still be the home of Jesus as it was before the time of Blessed Mother Margaret and has been ever since, even during the dark days of persecution.

May this holy soul watch over her ancient home with its present holy occupants. May she likewise intercede for those who live in her Principality of Wales, that ere long they may return to the Faith of their forefathers.

✠ Francis,
　　　　Archbishop of Cardiff.

January 1st, 1936.

INTRODUCTION

TRULY beautiful is the history of the life of the holy Carmelite Margaret Mostyn as it is unfolded to us in this volume, and one rises from the study of it with feelings of admiration and gratitude—admiration of the saintliness of her life, and gratitude to the kindly providence of God which gave so great a spirit of piety, devotion and self-sacrifice to our old Catholic families.

As the life of Mother Margaret abounds with instances of private revelation, it will be useful to remind ourselves of the attitude of theologians in their teaching and of the faithful in their practice when in the presence of such divine manifestations. God may speak to His children in various ways. There is His own written word in the Bible. There is the teaching authority of His Church : there is the voice of conscience, or the guidance of His priests, and other such ways which belong to the ordinary course of His dealings with His creatures. But He need not stay the hand of His special providence, nor remain silent in the case of certain chosen servants to whom He entrusts special tasks, and whose contact with others He wishes to be particularly fruitful. Thus we have the ' showings ' of Juliana of Norwich, the voices of Joan of Arc, the dreams of John Bosco, and the like, in all of which examples the devout reader is convinced and believes that the voice of God has spoken through the instrument of His choice.

One is not convinced, however, by reading of these things in isolation. One must study them in the framework of the whole life of the servant of God. Then we can view the beauty of the colour and perspective and are able to see how the intimate dealings of the Most High with the child of His hands are a most fitting complement to a life whose godliness calls forth our admiration.

Those who reflect on the beautiful life of Margaret Mostyn will feel that they are in the presence of a chosen soul in whom God was well pleased. The communications or showings which are related in her manuscript, carefully and devotedly preserved in the Carmel at Darlington, give forth the true ring of sound theological teaching. The person herself, humble, detached, self-effacing, childlike, reluctant to make known what had passed between her soul and God, charmingly simple in all her dealings with Him, excludes at once the suggestion of mere pious imaginings or fantastic dreamings. Then the fruit of her life in that community in which she spent her life as subject and superior, gives evidence of the wholesome nature of the tree on which it was ripened; and the flowers of her virtue were gathered gratefully by her sisters in religion, themselves 'lilies among which the Beloved found His nourishment.' The intimate relationship which Margaret enjoyed with God is described, often in her own words, with a delightful simplicity, and the pages are full of passages strikingly beautiful. Such, for example, are the revelation made to her by Our Lady of a devotion to her virtues in Chapter VII, the simple instruction concerning dispositions for Holy Communion in Chapter VI, her devotion to Our Lord's infancy, her childlike dealings with her heavenly Mother, her reverence for the priesthood of Jesus Christ, perpetuated in the priests of Holy Church.

Then there are messages from God with regard to the holiness of life required in His priests and the insistence (how often found in the revelations made to other holy souls !) that the more holy the minister the more blessed is the ministry, and the greater the radiance of light and heat to the souls whom God brings within the range of His influence. One catches, too, a vivid glimpse of Purgatory, and, in reading of Mother Margaret's experiences, one is sharply reminded of the probability that the souls of kith and kin and of the friends of other days are looking longingly for our prayers and good works whereby they may be happily gathered to the place of refreshment, light and peace.

So, in a variety of ways, and with unfailing charm, does the life of Margaret Mostyn speak to us and lift our souls to God. We Catholics do not bring forward such revelations as proofs of Catholic teaching, but the devout soul will feel here the presence of a great servant of God, and will know that he may prudently and piously believe.

I like to think that in the period of her life, 1625–1679, a time of storm and stress for her own country, lives such as hers, lived ' beyond the seas ' by girls who had left all to follow the Divine Master, helped our martyrs to climb to gallows with nimble step, or to pass the merry jest while the rope was about their neck, or to remain steadfast when the knife of the executioner was dripping with the blood of young men who themselves had put on the priesthood of Christ, beyond the seas. Thus it is with gratitude that I read of the miraculous recovery of Mother Margaret attributed to the intercession of Blessed Henry Morse, who was a student in the Venerable College at Rome, where I am writing these lines, and within whose walls he prepared for his future passion at Tyburn. And by a happy coincidence, maybe not without significance, I recall his death on the anniversary of his martyrdom, which took place on February 1st, 1645. Once, when Margaret was sick, the religious bethought themselves of a picture which Blessed Henry, on his way to martyrdom, had taken from his breviary and sent to the Prioress of the Carmel at Antwerp, as a token of his affection, with the following message :

' Remember me to those good religious and tell them when I come to heaven, whatsoever they shall ask of me, if it be pleasing to God, I will obtain it for them.' The picture was placed on Margaret's breast and the patient recovered her health.

Most interesting, too, is the message from the great St. Teresa of Avila that she has a special interest in England and is desirous to help in a particular way those English people who have recourse to her. Margaret Mostyn loved her native land. A glance at the history of those years which made up her life will reveal to us the noble sacrifices made by our holy martyrs in that dark, yet glorious, period. But let us, as we read, turn our thoughts from the rack and the torture-chamber, from the gallows and the cauldron and the blood, to the quiet cloisters of Carmel and of other houses of God where souls such as those of Margaret and her sisters held up their hands in prayer, and helped, in their own way, to make the victory possible. May its fruits be gathered more and more and vocations be multiplied, so that the daughters of St. Teresa may spread their prayerful influence throughout the land we love so well!

WILLIAM GODFREY.

VENERABLE ENGLISH COLLEGE,
    ROME,
        February 1st, 1936.

In an article by *Nestor* (Rt. Rev. Abbot Hunter Blair) in the *Catholic Times* for March 11th, 1932, it is stated that three months after his restoration Charles II ' conferred a baronetcy of England on Roger, heir of the line of Richard ap Howell ap Jevan Vychan, whose two sons, Thomas of Mostyn and Pyers of Talacre, assumed the surname of Moston, or Mostyn.' Mostyn Hall is situated on the banks of the Dee, south-east of Talacre, and north-west of Holywell. Sir Roger's male descendants became extinct, but are represented in the female line by Baron Mostyn of Mostyn, who is paternally a Lloyd. Thus Mother Margaret's family was ennobled during her lifetime, but long before that the Mostyns had been noted Catholic landowners in North Wales. They were connected by marriage with Owen Tudor, grandfather to King Henry VII, and once when, as Harry Richmond, the future King of England was captured by Yorkists, it was from Mostyn Hall that he escaped, through a hiding place still called the King's Hole. After the victory of Bosworth, Henry Tudor gave Mostyn the sword and belt that he had himself worn on the battle-field, and pressed him to come to Court. ' Sire (replied Mostyn), I dwell, and will dwell among my own people.' The spirit which prompted this reply is one of the strongest assets of this truly Catholic family, of which the cadet branch of Talacre has given, within the last century, two bishops to the Catholic Church : Francis George Mostyn, son of the fifth baronet, was appointed by Pope Gregory XVI Vicar Apostolic of the *Northern District* of England and Wales, and was consecrated Bishop of Abydus on December 21st, 1840. He died seven years later at the comparatively early age of forty-seven; in 1895, when Wales (except Glamorganshire) was erected into a separate Vicariate Apostolic, Francis Joseph Mostyn was chosen to govern it, his titular see being that of Ascalon. He is now Archbishop of Cardiff and Metropolitan of the Welsh Principality. Thus intimately is the name of Mostyn bound up with the return of the Faith to Wales. The family seat at Talacre is now the home of Benedictine nuns, formerly the Anglican community of Malling, founded in 1868 by Mother Hilda Stewart, which removed to St. Brides', Milford Haven, in April, 1911. Two years later, Bishop Mostyn (then of Menevia) had the consolation of receiving the whole community into the Catholic Church. After a year's probation, during which two nuns from Stanbrook lived at St. Brides' in order to train the newly received converts in the observances of regular Benedictine life, the Bishop installed Mother Scholastica (Mother Hilda Stewart's successor) as first Abbess, and a fortnight later, June 14th, 1914, received the vows of the community, not a single member having hesitated to follow where Mother Scholastica led.

In 1920 the nuns removed to Talacre, which had been put up for sale, and thus has it come about that the home where Margaret Mostyn must have played as a child has passed into the keeping of those who will cherish its Catholic memories and traditions. In its grounds was planted many years ago a young sapling, now known as ' Mother Margaret's Tree.'

Margaret was such a lovable child that her grandmother insisted upon bringing her up in her own house in Hurst, so that for the first fourteen or fifteen years of her life she could only have paid flying visits to Talacre. She must have been a lonely little girl, and often amused herself by gathering flowers to place before a picture of Our Lady with the Infant Jesus in her arms, or adorning it with bracelets, chains, and other jewelry. One day she was so busily occupied doing this that she forgot her dinner. She prattled to Our Lady of all her childish joys and sorrows, dailing asking her heavenly Mother's blessing, and reciting her Rosary, and Mary, in return, promised to take her under special protection. Margaret was of a timorous disposition, and in order to help her to overcome her fears, a Jesuit, who lived at Hurst, used to send her in the dark to fetch things from the most distant rooms in the house. In spite of her nervousness Margaret never refused, and often God rewarded her obedience and courage by allowing her to see her Angel Guardian, who sometimes led her by the hand, and sometimes carried her. This favour lasted till she was about twelve years old, and Margaret ever afterwards had a tender devotion to her Angel Guardian and to those of others. The little girl's faith was so vivid that once, when her grandmother was receiving Holy Communion, Margaret saw the Infant Jesus in the Sacred Host, and begged so hard to be allowed to receive Him that she had to be carried out of chapel. Another time she went alone on Holy Thursday to visit the Altar of Repose. Having lifted a chair close to the Blessed Sacrament, she was climbing up to the Chalice when someone chanced to come in and, lifting her down, asked what she was trying to do. ' I wanted to see my dear little Jesus,' she said. God called Margaret to be His bride while she was still a child, but old Mrs. Fox was determined not to let her go. In those days English Catholics who wanted to enter a religious Order had to go abroad to do so, and though priests might return as missionaries at the peril of their lives, nuns had to live in perpetual exile. Still, Margaret hoped to gain her grandmother's consent. It happened that her great-uncle, Mr. Layton, a holy old man who had lost his sight, used to spend long hours in prayer in the Hurst Chapel, where Margaret also went often to pray. She would sometimes interrupt his devotions with a request that he would intercede for her with her grandmother, for she feared if she delayed too long she might lose her vocation. Mr. Layton only smiled at his great-niece's eagerness, and put her off by telling her she was not ' cut out for a nun.' At that time Margaret had not made her First Communion, and when she was at last admitted to the Holy Table she again saw Our Lord in the consecrated particle, this time under the figure of the Good Shepherd, and felt her desire of being a religious deepened and strengthened. Her confessor, strange to relate, opposed her longing to give herself wholly to God, and even threatened not to allow her to go to Holy Communion again for a long time if she did not abandon her idea. Her grandmother also remained firm in her opposition, and to wean Margaret from her vocation, gave her the entire charge of the household. Considering Margaret's age, and the fact that several near relatives of maturer years were living at Hurst, this might have proved very awkward, especially as Mrs. Fox was growing daily more infirm. But the young girl, by her virtue and natural charm, won all hearts. Life went on peacefully under her rule, and in spite of her many duties Margaret found time for prayer, spiritual reading and instructing the domestic servants. Some of these were non-Catholics, but it speaks volumes for their trustworthiness that they were admitted to attend Mass, the ceremonies of which Margaret duly explained, and two of their number were at their own request fully instructed by her in the Catholic Faith, and received into the Church.

Day by day old Mrs. Fox grew weaker. Margaret waited upon her day and night, for though two strong maids had her in their constant care, nothing was done to the old lady's satisfaction unless her granddaughter had a hand in it. Just before the end, when the Last Sacraments had been administered, the dying woman called Margaret to her side and thanked her for the 'cheerful and faithful' attendance she had bestowed upon her, begging her forgiveness for hindering her entrance into religion. When her grandmother had been laid to rest, there was no longer any reason why Margaret should remain at Hurst. Her father had died some time before and Mrs. Mostyn, who was living at Greenfield, about a mile N.N.E. of Holywell, on the left bank of the river Dee, was glad to have her daughter at home to help in the management of the household. At first the idea of becoming a nun still haunted Margaret, and she felt herself torn between love for her mother and an interior call to a more perfect following of Our Lord. Once again she consulted her confessor, who advised her to put aside all thought of being a religious and enter whole-heartedly into the innocent pleasures of her life at home. By degrees she grew to like gay company and the amusements of life in the country, and even left off her custom of spiritual reading lest it should remind her of God's call. She could not bear to hear the word 'nun' and tried by every means she could think of to drown the voice of conscience which told her she was made for better things than the pleasures and happiness enjoyed by those around her. During this time, a deep and lasting friendship grew up between Margaret and her youngest sister, Elizabeth. The latter had lived amid the companionship of brothers and sisters, and Mrs. Mostyn had seen to it that they were all well instructed in the doctrine and practice of the Catholic Faith. Like Margaret, Elizabeth had a special love of Our Blessed Lady. There was a chapel at Greenfield which, though then in a ruinous state, had formerly been a centre of devotion to the Blessed Virgin, under whose invocation it had been dedicated. Here little Elizabeth frequently led her playmates to offer prayers in honour of the Mother of God. One favourite devotion consisted in creeping round the inside of the ruined chapel on bare knees by way of penance and mortification. On the feast of Our Lady's Assumption, 1637, Elizabeth made her first Communion, and felt inspired to dedicate herself for ever to the service of God. At this the devil raised doubts in her heart, which were only quelled when Our Lady appeared to her, clothed in radiant white, and assured her that she already belonged to her, and that the solemn promise she proposed making would render her still more pleasing in God's sight and her own. Elizabeth thereupon pledged herself to become a nun, and, for three years, quiet, peaceful happiness dwelt in her soul. Her mother, knowing nothing of all this, proposed an advantageous marriage to her when she was fourteen. Elizabeth answered that she had promised herself to God, and refused to entertain any other idea.

Mrs. Mostyn sent her to the family confessor, who made light of her promise and told her to give it up. For a time Elizabeth tried to stifle her conscience, and, when Margaret came to live at Greenfield, the two sisters used to wander together about the grounds, sharing each other's secrets on all matters except that of their call to religious life. Margaret, seeing Elizabeth apparently gay and happy, could not bear the thought of parting from her, and Elizabeth made Margaret promise that she would never go away and leave her behind. They hid their real desire by planning that, if one got married, the other should try to find for a husband some gentleman living in the same neighbourhood, so that they should still be near each other.

Yet in their hearts, both were ill at ease. God's voice was insistent, and at last Margaret could not bear to be alone lest she should have to give heed to it and be obliged to leave all for His sake. Doubt, fear and longing fought for mastery in her soul, and neither she nor Elizabeth were really happy. No matter how gay the company of which she formed part, Margaret invariably found it palling upon her, and she would withdraw in disgust and try to distract herself by reading idle books, or else took refuge in work.

On one such occasion she left the family circle and went alone into the garden, where she walked about aimlessly, wrestling with herself. Suddenly Our Blessed Lady stood in the pathway before her and, looking compassionately upon her, said : ' My child, if thou wilt be happy, follow thy first vocation. St. Teresa will help thee.'

Startled as she was by this vision, Margaret never doubted its reality, and all her hesitation vanished. Her soul was flooded with peace, and she began to plan means of obeying Our Lady's injunction. The devil raised all kinds of obstacles, not the least of which was the promise she had made to Elizabeth, which he represented as binding in conscience. For two months Margaret delayed, but one day, as she entered the chapel to make her usual devotions, Our Lady again appeared to her, telling her to inform her confessor that she wished to be a Discalced Carmelite, and also to tell Elizabeth, who, the Blessed Mother assured her, was likewise called to the same Order.

Margaret obeyed at once. This time the confessor made no objection, and, to her intense surprise, neither did Elizabeth, who at once confided to Margaret her own experiences in the matter. Now at last the two sisters could open their hearts to each other without restraint.

They began that very day to study a book, *On the Happiness of the Religious State*, by Father Jerome Platus, which Elizabeth had caused to be put away lest she should yield to its pleading of Christ's cause. Together they told their mother that their minds were finally made up, and she no longer opposed their desire. Nevertheless, it took a year to complete all arrangements for their going abroad.

During that time Margaret had several proposals of marriage, especially from one suitor, 'who thought his pretensions could meet with no refusal,' as the old chronicle puts it. Finding his attentions disregarded, he made use of charms to obtain the satisfaction of his passion. Though Margaret was wholly innocent of any participation in such forbidden practices, her being thus involved in them caused her acute distress, and as a consequence she suffered much in body and in mind, not only at the time, but for many years afterwards. In expiation for this, and for her long delay in corresponding to the graces showered upon her, Margaret now divided her day between penance and prayer. She had at last put her hand to the plough, and never looked back. She was at this time only about eighteen, Elizabeth a year younger, and as the Civil War was at its height, and travelling through England dangerous, especially to members of such a well-known Royalist family, it was decided that the chaplain at Greenfield should accompany them as well as their brother Edward, with the necessary number of servants. Weymouth was chosen as the port of embarkation, chiefly because it had remained faithful to the King.

The party travelled by unfrequented roads in order to avoid meeting any Parliamentarian troops, and, with many narrow escapes, they reached Weymouth without mishap.

The two girls thought the worst dangers were over, but they had to wait for the ship, and in the interval the town was surrounded by Cromwell's

Roundheads, who cut off all communication with
the sea. A change of plan became an imperative
necessity. It happened that Lord Arundell of
Wardour,[1] with a company of cavalry, was posted
at Weymouth for the purpose of escorting Queen
Henrietta Maria to Exeter. Edward Mostyn
obtained leave for his party to join them, for, had
he been discovered, both his life and estates would
have been forfeited. Margaret opposed this new
arrangement with all the energy of which she was
capable, and kept urging her brother to put his
trust in God. After much discussion it was decided
to let Margaret determine what should be done. She
immediately asked all present to kneel down and
recite the Litany of the Blessed Virgin, after which
each member of the party should decide as he
thought best. While they were at their prayers,
news was secretly brought that there lay at anchor
some distance outside Weymouth harbour, a loyal
frigate, which was due to sail that night with des-
patches for Holland. This decided the matter. As
soon as it grew dark, a party of four set off from the
inn and walked unhindered to the shore, though the
town was in an uproar, and reached the boat which
was to take them to the frigate. A sentinel standing
near noticed them pushing off and called a challenge.
Receiving no answer, he raised his musket, but could
not get it to take fire. Three times he applied the
match, with no result. This unwonted failure
struck the man, who was of a religious turn of mind,
and he called out : ' Go, in God's name, for He is

[1] Thomas, second Lord Arundell, killed at the battle of
Lansdowne, May 19th, 1643. His wife, Blanche, led the
famous defence of Wardour Castle just a fortnight earlier.

surely with you, otherwise you had perished ! ' The gentlemen pulled at the oars, and before long the travellers were safely aboard the frigate. Danger still lay ahead, for the Parliamentary fleet blocked the harbour. All fell to their prayers, and the captain managed to steer his vessel through the hostile ships into the English Channel.

By some ill-chance news spread of the departure of Royalists, to whom travel of any kind was forbidden by Cromwell, with the result that the friendly boat was chased by two hostile swift-sailing frigates. These were descried some miles distant at dawn the following morning, and the Royalist captain altered his course for France, since, as he assured his passengers, his frigate could not out-distance its pursuers, and he must either fight against overwhelming odds or sink his ship, which had, moreover, sprung a leak. Margaret and Elizabeth were terrified, but kept praying to Our Lady that they might not have to return to England. She appeared to them as they knelt huddled together, and comforted them by saying that they belonged to her and she would keep them safe. That same evening her promise was fulfilled, for quite unex-pectedly their boat entered the Bay of Havre de Grâce,[1] where a portion of the French fleet lay at anchor. All day their pursuers had pressed hard upon them, but the sight of the French ships caused them to turn back. The extraordinary nature of this escape made the captain wonder who his passengers might be, but as they were all in disguise,

[1] Literally, The Harbour of Grace. It was a simple fishing village, with a chapel dedicated to Our Lady of Grace, until 1516, when Francis I constructed its harbour.

they thought it wiser not to make themselves known for his sake as well as on their own account, and, instead of accompanying him to Holland, determined to make the rest of their journey by land.

Being in need of rest, they stayed a few days at Havre. It was a new experience to be able to go openly to Mass, and the two girls were eager to see as much as they could, especially of convents and nuns. While they were praying about their journey, Our Lady appeared to them. This time she told them not to be discouraged by any difficulties, for she would protect them for the rest of their way as she had done on their way to Havre. A venerable old priest whom they saw in the Convent there, gravely told them that he knew that they were going to be Teresian nuns. This astonished them very much, but so many English girls crossed over to the Continent at that period in order to give themselves to God, that if the old priest knew their destination to be Antwerp, it was not an unlikely conclusion for him to come to. The same thing happened when they broke their journey overland at Pontoise. There they visited the Carmelite Convent where the prioress, a daughter of Blessed Marie de l'Incarnation Acarie, received them with great kindness, even offering to accept Margaret and Elizabeth without dowries as members of her community. The two girls endeavoured to conceal their intention of becoming nuns, but the holy prioress evidently knew the truth, for she set their explanation aside. ' I know very well,' she said, ' that you will both become nuns, and nuns of our Holy Order.' Soon the travellers were on the

road again. It was mid-July and the heat was
intense. Somewhere between Pontoise and Antwerp
a thoroughly Teresian incident took place. As the
coach lumbered on with its four occupants, Edward
felt he could bear the heat no longer, and proposed
getting out to walk. He gave the order to the driver,
but before the clumsy vehicle could be brought to a
halt, he tried to jump out and, in doing so, slipped
and fell under the rear wheel, which passed right
over his body. His sisters thought he was killed,
and clambered out quickly to go to his aid. What
was their surprise to see him pick himself up before
they had time to reach him. He had neither bruise
nor scar, though a rent in his clothes testified to the
truth of the accident. All four thanked Our Lord
and His Blessed Mother for so wonderful an escape.

As the travellers drew nearer to Antwerp
Margaret's fears and doubts returned, but once they
had arrived and knelt in the small Carmelite church
to give thanks for their preservation through so
many perils, all her diffidence vanished, and she and
Elizabeth could think and talk of nothing but their
approaching reception as Discalced Carmelite
novices. The English Carmel in Hopland, Antwerp,
was in August, 1644, the time of the Mostyn's
arrival, still governed by its first prioress, Mother
Anne of the Ascension (Worsley), who was regarded
as its foundress and who had during her rule of
twenty-six years clothed forty-eight English ladies
with the habit of Our Lady of Mount Carmel.
Margaret and Elizabeth Mostyn brought the number
up to fifty. On the feast of St. Lawrence (August
10th) they entered the church, dressed as brides
and adorned with priceless jewels lent for the

occasion by Lady Catherine Howard and the Countess of Arundel, who led them to their places. Mother Anne of the Ascension felt great interior consolation as she dressed the two sisters in the Carmelite habit and veil. This was especially the case while she was attending to Margaret, who, she felt, would do great good in the Order. Margaret herself was overwhelmed with happiness. Yet once again she saw the Infant Jesus in the consecrated host when Bishop Gaspar Nemins communicated her during Mass, and throughout the whole of the ceremony was comforted by seeing Our Lady standing on her right 'which neither change of posture, nor others that were stirring about her, were able to intercept or hinder.' Nothing further is told in the ancient chronicle about the return of Edward Mostyn and his chaplain to England. The farewells were bravely said, no doubt, on both sides, and Edward had a last look at his sisters behind the grate before he left them to the care of Mother Anne of the Ascension. Henceforth, Margaret was known as 'Margaret of Jesus,' Elizabeth, as 'Ursula of All Saints.'

CHAPTER II

IN THE ENGLISH CARMEL, ANTWERP
1644–1648

MOTHER ANNE of the Ascension soon realised that Sister Margaret and Sister Ursula were full of the spirit of St. Teresa. She called them her ' greatest treasures,' and wrote of Margaret to Düsseldorf :

' The eldest is endowed with such admirable parts and perfections, both of nature and grace, that she will be able to advance our Order greatly, which I would not have you look upon as written by way of compliment, but upon just and reasonable motives.'

At first Margaret found her new life very difficult. She had a natural aversion to fish and eggs (Carmelites eat no meat), and the mere handling of woollen stuff was disagreeable to her, so that she had plenty of opportunities of involuntary mortification, to which she added others of her own choosing, though her virtue enabled her to do all this without letting it be seen how much these trifles cost her. Her Guardian Angel encouraged her by sometimes appearing in visible form. About a month after Sister Margaret had received the habit of Mount Carmel, she noticed outside the window of her cell an apple tree loaded with green fruit. One apple fairer than the rest, caught her eye, and she thought how much she would like to gather it to eat. This she thought was a temptation to self-indulgence, and her will immediately responded. ' I will mortify myself in this (she said) for the love of God.' At that moment her Guardian Angel appeared, and, gathering the apple, seemed to turn it into a beautiful crown, assuring her at the same time that no action, however small, done for love of God, ever passed without its reward. Another story of Margaret's Guardian Angel, which belongs to her later life, may be given here. One day at Mass she was asking Saint Teresa to help her in preparing to keep her feast, when she suddenly felt the presence of her ' Good Angel,' as she called him.

> ' I cannot say I did see anything ' (she wrote later to her confessor), ' for my eyes were shut ; neither did I hear anything ; yet it seemed to me he said : " *Do what you do, and I will take care of the rest.*" ' Margaret added that from that day she referred everything to the care of her Guardian Angel, and so found herself ' out of pain with the event.'

The Mistress of Novices at that time was Mother Margaret of St. Teresa (Downes). She trained Margaret with special care, and provided occasions in which her virtue was put to the test, such as blaming her for some fault committed by another, which Sister Margaret bore quite cheerfully without attempting to excuse herself. Her greatest difficulty was with regard to prayer. She faithfully followed the method taught by her Novice-Mistress, but found herself unable to use either her imagination or

c

reasoning power to help towards colloquy with Our
Lord or His Blessed Mother. In great distress she
came to look upon her hours of prayer as so much
waste of time. Reflecting one day upon this
disability to meditate, Sister Margaret humbled
herself before the Divine Majesty, and adored God
present in her heart. Upon this she seemed to hear
Our Lord say : ' Here have I established my
dwelling.' From that time she no longer tried to
force herself into any special method of prayer, but
spent the time quietly dwelling upon some mystery
of Our Lord's life, or, when God withheld the
favours of this tacit union, she made acts of faith,
or thought out means of overcoming her faults and
of mortifying her natural inclinations.

Four months after their clothing, Sisters Margaret
and Ursula, with the rest of the community,
mourned the loss of Mother Anne of the Ascension,
who died in the odour of sanctity on December
23rd, 1644. During the interim, before a canonical
election of a new Mother Prioress could take place,
Sister Margaret underwent temptation concerning
the truth of her vocation. She was also anxious
about Sister Ursula, who was experiencing a
similar trial. Prostrate one day before the Blessed
Sacrament, Margaret was praying for herself and her
sister, when Our Lord appeared to her. He
comforted her, saying He would never forsake her,
but that Heaven could not be easily won. The trials
she was going through (He said) were permitted
for a greater good, and that the house, in spite of
certain faults which she had noticed in the nuns,
was one in which He would be well served. Finally,
He bade her confide in her confessor, assuring her

MARGARET MOSTYN BEFORE SHE ENTERED THE
ENGLISH CARMEL, ANTWERP, 1644
(From a portrait preserved at Carmel House, Darlington.)

grace and the greatest saint in Heaven. I am glorified in glorifying them, and I reward each soul according to its merit.' Our Lord then showed Sister Margaret in what manner the Saints differ in glory, namely, in a more or less clear sight and knowledge of God, so that those in a higher degree of glory, see and enjoy the glory of those below them, and the latter, though without knowing what the Saints who are above them are enjoying, nevertheless rejoice in their glory, which constantly gives them fresh delight.

' In the same manner, whatever I show thee (Our Lord explained) is always new, whether it be in itself greater or less, and thou dost always think it incomparable, and the same happens with My Saints in heaven. They always find My glory new, and surpassing anything they could imagine, though each saint enjoys it in a different degree, nor do they feel any envy because their happiness is to rejoice in My will and glory, which I make known by rewarding all men according to their merit. Some while on earth were more faithful in corresponding to My inspirations and in their labours for My glory, and in these, I am more seen and honoured both in time and throughout eternity.'

After this, Sister Margaret felt her soul placed in the presence of the Blessed Trinity and she understood better than before the mystery of the Incarnation, and how the merit and glory of the Saints were its fruit, and that there were as many Saints upon the earth then as there were in past times. Finally,

Our Lord showed her a book, and asked if she knew what it contained. Sister Margaret dared not answer, thinking it was the record of her sins. But Jesus, smiling sweetly upon her, opened it and ' showed her her vows written in a clear hand, and underneath them a little act which she was frequently accustomed to make : *Lord, what I have promised Thee is pleasing to me.*' These words were in brighter lettering than the rest, and Our Lord gently reproached her because through scrupulous fear she often omitted to repeat her vows, though she unconsciously renewed them by this little act, which Our Lord told her was written in the Book of Life, that is, in Himself. Thereupon, she saw her vows written, as it were, in Him, but ' with her usual act somewhat changed,' so that it read, ' *What thou hast promised to Me, is pleasing to Me.*' Our Lord then spoke to her heart :

' See now, I hope thou wilt ever esteem the vows of religion by which so much may be gained, for though religious persons should often offend Me, even by breaking their vows, yet if at their death they are in a state of grace, their places in Heaven will be above the angels, and merely in virtue of their vows they will be ranked next to priests. What then, dost thou think, will be the glory of a faithful soul who, possessed of this high prerogative, goes on daily advancing in perfection, seeking in everything to honour and please Me ? Let this be thy constant aim, not so much because thou shalt thereby see and enjoy Me more (which, however, is a very good intention), but because the more thou dost merit, the more dost thou glorify Me, which intention, as being the most perfect, will give more lustre to thine actions and render them more acceptable and pleasing to Me. By this, souls are purified from all self-interest and become more closely united to Almighty God, Who cannot fail to reward them with mutual love and all kinds of heavenly graces.'

Sister Margaret pondered deeply on what she had been shown, and resolved always to regulate her life by what Our Lord had told her. He encouraged her in this, at the same time warning her to set great value on little things, and esteem nothing small which could add to His honour and glory. As He said this, He seemed to increase in beauty and splendour, and so vanished from sight, leaving the young religious consoled and strengthened. On the morning of her profession, Our Lady appeared to Sister Margaret after she had received Holy Communion, inspiring her to become her slave by voluntarily renouncing all satisfaction she might feel in anything she did, and explaining the great reward attached to such an oblation. After some hesitation Margaret made this offering, and the Blessed Virgin immediately calmed her anxiety about it, and told her that, by bearing in mind all that her Divine Son suffered, she would get grace to be faithful to it.

It is needless to say that Margaret's faults and weaknesses were not got rid of by the mere fact of her becoming a Carmelite. She had a quick, sensitive disposition, and was often tempted to impatience. On one occasion something unkind that had

been said about her was repeated in her presence, and
Sister Margaret, deeply hurt, planned reprisals.
Suddenly, though she saw nothing, she heard a
voice saying : ' *Thou art not despised as I was !* '
Full of sorrow for her fault, she asked God's
forgiveness, and ever after strove to be particularly
kind to those who she knew felt less favourably
disposed towards her.

Her fear of the dark also remained, and in order
to overcome it she went alone into the dead-cellar
every evening after Compline, and there performed
devotions and penances for the souls in Purgatory.
She was not allowed to practise great austerities in
addition to those prescribed by the Carmelite Rule,
but she was very ingenious in finding ways of
mortifying her bodily senses, such as placing herself
in some uncomfortable posture in her cell and so
remaining, no matter how wearisome it grew, until
the bell rang for some community duty. After she
had been professed for some months, God sent the
trial of sickness. For twelve days she was in a state
of high fever, and the doctors, failing to diagnose
her disease, pronounced it incurable. This caused
great distress among her fellow-religious, and
particularly to those in authority, for they were
building great hopes that Sister Margaret would
become a holy and useful Superior. Many prayers
went up to Heaven that she might be spared, but
life seemed to be ebbing away. At this juncture one
of the nuns remembered Father Henry Morse's
promise on the day of his martyrdom, O.S. January
23rd, 1645. On that morning he had taken a
picture from his breviary, and giving it to Father
Thomas Worsley, S.J., who attended him the night

before and on the scaffold, said : ' Give this to Mother Prioress of Antwerp,[1] and remember me to those good nuns. Tell them that when I come to Heaven, whatsoever they shall ask of me, if it be pleasing to God and for their good, I will obtain it for them.' Upon this, the Mother Prioress (Anne of St. Augustine) assembled the community, and, while the Sisters invoked the holy martyr, she laid Father Morse's picture upon the dying nun's breast, and gave her a little wine mingled with a drop of his blood, of which they had a small quantity in a phial. Instantly the fever abated, and when the doctor came, expecting to find Sister Margaret dead, he was intensely astonished to see that she was out of danger. Nevertheless, the drastic remedies that had been applied left great weakness, and the young religious never regained complete health. All her life she suffered from severe head-aches, and her digestion was so impaired that she could retain scarcely any food, and for some months lived solely on raw orange peel. As soon as she could drag herself about, she begged to be allowed to follow the usual community routine, and could not bear to be dispensed from any duty.

When she was a little stronger she was made infirmarian. It was a difficult charge, for at that time there was an unusual number of Sisters in the English Carmel. Negotiations for a new foundation were in progress and there were practically two

---

[1] Mother Anne of the Ascension, who was, so far as is known, Fr. Worsley's eldest sister. The news of her death on the 23rd of the previous December had not then reached England.

communities living together, which brought the number of nuns up to forty. In addition to this, there was a confirmed invalid, Sister Dorothy, for whom Sister Margaret had everything to do, and whose infirmities rendered her very irritable. Outwardly Sister Margaret was a devoted nurse, but often enough her natural feelings revolted at her many disagreeable tasks, until one day she was rebuked by her Guardian Angel, who told her that, if she could not continue her kind offices for the poor suffering Sister, he would undertake them for her. ' Didst thou but know the beauty of that Sister's soul (he said), thou wouldst think it the greatest blessing on earth to be near her.' Thus encouraged, Sister Margaret found easy what before had been so difficult. She nursed the invalid untiringly day and night until her death, and was afterwards assured by Our Blessed Lady that Sister Dorothy had merited greater glory by her hidden, suffering life than had many other deceased persons who had been, while on earth, esteemed for their sanctity. During this period Sister Margaret, who was very busy all day, once or twice omitted to say the *Ave Maria* when Carmelite custom required it. On one occasion she heard her Guardian Angel reciting it, and he told her that such devotions performed with a spirit of obedience were often more acceptable to God than great penances and other extraordinary works.

In a paper written by her own hand, the young infirmarian lets us know that she was a little troubled at receiving this important charge, for she had strong likes and dislikes, and felt herself easily distracted by exterior work.

' I will endeavour to serve Christ Our Lord in the sick (she wrote), doing all things concerning them in the same manner as I would do actually to the person of Our Blessed Lord.'

She also relates that Our Lord told her that if she did this, all would become easy. ' I have brought thee here (He said), to love Me and Me only. Thou must not incline to those for whom thou hast inclination or contradiction, but behold them all in Me.' And she adds :

' To the best that I know of myself I have not lost [by being infirmarian], for whether I will or no, I find myself carry a reverence to the Sacred Humanity of Christ Our Lord in all persons, and this causes recollection in me as long as it lasts.'

On the same paper is a note to the effect that often people are more secure in times of great danger and temptation than when assailed by petty failings such as curiosity, breaking silence and lack of custody of the eyes. These, usually looked upon as trifling imperfections, are in reality great hindrances to spiritual progress because less effort is made in regard to them than is the case with more apparent spiritual dangers.

It was during this period of her life that Sister Margaret was visited by a soul in Purgatory. The account is graphically given by Canon Bedingfeld :

' Upon an Ascension Eve, at night, having been during the day employed and much fatigued in serving the sick, Sister Margaret of Jesus was sent to her cell to take her rest. She had not been

there long before she suddenly heard herself
called upon by her worldly name, " *Miss Mostyn*."
As she knew all the Sisters were in choir she was
much frightened, but after some little consideration, having blessed herself with the sign of the
Cross, she rose up and opened her door to see if
there was anyone about who wanted her. Finding all quiet and nothing to be seen, she returned
again to her bed, in which she had scarce composed herself when she heard her religious name
twice repeated very distinctly. This gave her a
new uneasiness. However, she endeavoured to
pacify herself, thinking it might only be apprehension, and let it pass without saying anything
till at length it grew so constant that she was
every night wakened and frightened, sometimes
by noises in her cell, sometimes by rustling of
papers, and sometimes a cold air would blow
upon her as sensibly as if someone had made use
of a pair of bellows. When these disturbances
were past, her fear immediately ceased, which
made the thing appear more wonderful, and,
having casually spoken of it to some of the nuns,
they advised her to tell the Reverend Mother.
This she did, and the Prioress thereupon ordered
her to change her cell and appointed some
religious to watch by her at night ; yet, still
about the same hour, Sister Margaret was
awakened and frightened as usual.

' Upon this, the Reverend Mother consulted
the confessor, who gave orders that Sister
Margaret should speak to the spirit, for he was
convinced that it must needs be more than fancy.
For greater security, and to diminish her appre-

hension, she was laid in the upper choir before the Blessed Sacrament, and the sub-prioress, Mother Margaret of St. Teresa, being looked upon as one of the most courageous, was appointed to watch by her, accompanied by another Sister, and to give her the words lest through fright she should forget them. When the time came, which was always between twelve and one, she was suddenly awakened, according to custom, trembling with fear. After a little pause she was able to say the words after the sub-prioress, which were these : " In the Name of God, if you have leave, show what you would have." Immediately was represented to her a book with her own handwriting in it, and signed with her name, which made the whole story clear in an instant, for in the twinkling of an eye she was gone.'

The spirit was that of a maidservant who had waited upon Margaret at Hurst, and who had died three or four years before she had gone to the English Carmel. Though an excellent maid, with ' an extraordinary genius for dressing ladies according to the mode,' she was melancholy and scrupulous and tormented herself with all kinds of doubts when the dressing was done. One day she had spent a long time dressing Margaret, when a Jesuit Father who lived in the house came into the room, and she began to lay her scruples before him.

' But he (says the chronicle) being desirous of having her mistress speedily with him, without listening further to her ditty, told her that if she would only make haste he would pray her out of Purgatory, and promised three Masses. There-

known what Our Lady had said to her, only to be told that she herself was not among those proposed for the new Carmel, but that her sister Elizabeth had been chosen. 'I had hoped (the Prioress said) that you would endeavour to persuade your sister to go.' 'I know full well that my sister will never agree to be separated from me (Sister Margaret answered), but since Your Reverence desires it, I will not fail to propose it to her.'

Before speaking to Sister Ursula, Margaret consulted her confessor, Father Andrew White, a very holy man. She had already told him of what Our Lady had desired her to do, and he was wholly opposed to her leaving Antwerp. Now, however, she found him changed. He assured her that while offering Mass he had had a special light upon the matter. It was now clear to him that it was God's will that she should go to the new foundation, which would be greatly to His honour and her own good.

'All this gave her a better heart (says the chronicle) and diminished the reluctance she had to quit her mother-monastery, but she was much perplexed how to bring things about with her sister, till Our Blessed Lady, after her accustomed manner, appeared to her and confirmed all that her confessor had said,' adding that the new Carmel ' was the directed way to Heaven for her, no less than to her sister, and that it would be a house wholly dedicated to her service.'

Thus reassured, Margaret sought out her sister, and told her everything. When Ursula heard the words of Our Lady quoted above, she remembered that she too had had a vision of Our Lady on St. Teresa's eve the previous year. The Blessed Virgin had reproached her ' for a certain conversation she had kept with one of the nuns,' and told her ' she might prepare herself to be removed to another house where she (Our Lady) would be well served.'

This made decision easy. Sister Margaret at once went back to the Prioress and told her that she and Ursula were willing to leave Antwerp. Mother Teresa of Jesus accepted their offer, but enjoined them not so much as to mention the matter to anyone until she gave leave. This was a great privation, especially to Sister Margaret, whose nature was very affectionate and sensitive, nor was she wholly able to dissemble her grief at so sudden a departure, for the list of names for the new foundation was to be read only three days before the Sisters' departure. Sometimes when speaking to those nuns whom she particularly felt leaving, she could not refrain from tears, and they, not having the least idea of what was about to take place, wondered what they had done to hurt her. However, Margaret struggled bravely to overcome herself, and, helped by prayer, she so far succeeded that

' when the names were publicly read, she found her difficulties to leave her friends not so great as she had imagined, but became rather ashamed of her seeming insensibility, not expressing the least trouble to leave those who were the most solicitous (out of kindness for her) to keep her amongst them, not listening to any reasons they could allege to dissuade her from abandoning her mother-house.'

Three days later, namely, on August 26th, 1648, nine choir nuns, one novice, and two lay-sisters, set out for Lierre, where the new foundation was to be made. Mother Teresa of Jesus went with them, as did also the Vicar-General of the diocese of Antwerp. Thus came to an end the four happy years spent by Margaret and her sister in the first English Carmel.

D

CHAPTER III

THE FOUNDATION IN LIERRE

AUGUST, 1648–1651

THE foundation of a second exclusively English Carmel in Lierre was only accomplished, say the Lanherne Annals, 'with unspeakable trouble.' This was partly on account of a Royal Edict, issued some years previously, which forbade the establishment of new religious foundations in the Netherlands. In spite of the difficulties and persecution which beset Catholics in England at this time, a steady stream of young people continually crossed the Channel to become priests, monks and nuns. In 1647 the English Carmel alone counted forty in community, and as this number far exceeded the limit set by St. Teresa, another foundation became an imperative necessity. Those who came from England at the risk of their lives in order to consecrate themselves to God could not be sent back, nor refused what they so humbly and ardently craved. Consequently, Mother Teresa of Jesus (Ward), then Prioress in Hopland, entered into negotiations with the Bishop of Antwerp, Mgr Gaspar Nemins, who laid the matter before the secular authorities.

'The Reformed Order of Carmel was then in such repute in these countries[1] (says the ancient

[1] The Spanish Netherlands.

34

chronicle) that, provided they [the Carmelite nuns] had licence from the Court, most towns were ready to receive them with open arms, each thinking it a happiness to have thereof within their walls. Such were the dispositions of the citizens of Lierre, who readily acquiesced in the pious representations of their virtuous prelate, and assured him they were willing to admit the said religious upon condition that they should not be in any ways burthensome to the town by begging, or any ways molest the burghers thereof by their building or enclosure.'

Lierre lies within the diocese of Antwerp, and Bishop Nemins, on behalf of the nuns, used all his interest with the Archduke Leopold, then Governor of the Netherlands, to obtain leave for the proposed foundation. He succeeded so well that the Archduke not only granted the English nuns a licence to found, but also recommended them to the favour of the clergy and magistrates of Lierre. Thereupon the bishop himself wrote to the civic authorities, communicating to them the Archduke's approval and warmly commending the nuns, all of whom he knew personally, for he often visited the English Carmel in Hopland.

After this, final arrangements were soon made. The magistrates of Lierre had a document ' drawn up in proper form, signed and sealed and given to the religious as a security for their admittance, after having been registered in the books of the town.'

Meanwhile, Bishop Nemins had some difficulty in finding a chaplain for the new community. It happened that Father Edmund Bedingfeld, a

young English priest, was making a passing visit
to Antwerp at that time, and he was invited to the
episcopal palace, where the bishop asked him if he
would be willing to escort the nuns to Lierre and
act as their chaplain until some English-speaking
priest could be found for the post.

Several members of the Bedingfeld family were
nuns in the various English Convents in the
Netherlands, two cousins to Father Edmund having
been professed in Hopland, though in 1648 they
were both in Düsseldorf, where a Carmel had been
founded in 1643. After some hesitation, Father
Edmund accepted the bishop's proposal. Though
later on he was made Canon of St. Gomare's
Church, he remained with the Carmelites in Lierre
until his death in 1680. The nuns' chronicle says :

'His disinterestedness was extraordinary, for
although he served the community gratis and
entirely at his own expense as to victuals, lodging
and other necessaries, for the space of thirty-two
years, he could never be prevailed on to receive
any small presents they were often out of gratitude solicitous to give him.'

Canon Bedingfeld spent the major part of his
private income in assisting the Carmel in Lierre.
In their gratitude for his numerous benefactions the
nuns wrote a short account of his life, which is
included in their necrology :

'Our most dear and worthy confessor (it
reads) called Edmund Bedingfeld, native of
England, was born at Oxburgh in the county of

Norfolk, on the 13th August in the year 1615, son to Henry Bedingfeld, Knight, and his wife Elizabeth Hantin.'

After studying at St. Omer and Liége, Edmund returned home for three months, where he won his father's reluctant consent to study for the priesthood. After completing his theological course in the Netherlands he was ordained priest on St. Stephen's Day, and not long after went to Rome. There the Cardinal Protector offered him preferments, but he had no desire for important offices, and found his way back to the Netherlands, living first at Liége and then in Brussels. In order that he might be better able to help the Carmelites he accepted a Canonry of St. Gomare. All through his life Canon Bedingfeld had a deep devotion to Our Blessed Lady, and it was because he recognized that Discalced Carmelites are very specially ' daughters of the Blessed Virgin ' that he consented to become Chaplain at Lierre. He died on September 4th, 1680, and was buried in the Lady Chapel of St. Gomare's Church. The English Carmelites put a marble stone over his grave, and

' against the pillar is set also (their) glorious Mother's image with the Seraph piercing her heart, and his coat arms at her feet, that all may know how much he had done for her honour and the service of this Convent.'

In 1648 everything seemed favourable, and the twelve Sisters with their escort arrived safely in Lierre during the afternoon of August 26th. They went at once to the house which had been rented

for a temporary convent, and there the first check
awaited them. Says the chronicle :

> ' They repaired immediately to a house they
> had agreed for, but unexpectedly finding the
> owners thereof run from their bargain, and ready
> to drive them away with threats that if they
> made pretension to it, they would soon find
> means to break their intended foundation, the
> poor nuns were obliged peaceably and patiently
> to retire to a large house, which, after some
> inquiries, they had found in a bye-corner of the
> town at that time casually empty.'

This first refuge of the Carmelites in Lierre was
the inalienable property of a neighbouring Abbey of
Bernardine Dames called ' *Nazareth*,' which Mother
Teresa of Jesus hired ' at the rate of four hundred
florins a year, till such time as an occasion offered
of purchasing another more to their liking and
convenience.' Meanwhile, the Carmelites were
allowed to make whatever alterations were necessary, but it was nearly six weeks before these were
sufficiently advanced for a chapel to be fitted up
where the Blessed Sacrament could be reserved.
The Carmel was dedicated ' To Our Blessed Lady
of Mount Carmel and St. Joseph,' and the formal
opening took place on October 4th, the feast of
St. Francis of Assisi. This Saint afterwards revealed
to Sister Margaret of Jesus that he had taken the
Convent under his particular protection. The
chronicle adds that,

> ' the ceremony was performed with all the
> solemnity their poor circumstances would per-
> mit, and attended by a concourse of devout

people who, as they gradually grew acquainted with the house, became also admirers of the spirit of poverty, mortification and patience which remarkably appeared in all they saw or heard of it, so that the Community gained the repute of sanctity and was spoken of by all with the greatest veneration.'

The Sisters who formed this first community at Lierre are still revered by their successors now at Darlington. Besides the two Mostyns there were Mother Margaret of St. Teresa (Downes) (Vicaress), Catherine of the Blessed Sacrament (Windoe), Mary Anne of Jesus (Foster), Mary of Jesus (Powderle), Elizabeth of the Visitation (Emery), Eugenia of Jesus (Leveson), Hieronima of St. Michael (Winter), Mary of St. Joseph (Vaughan) (novice) and two lay-sisters, Margaret of St. Francis (Johnson) and Alexis of St. Winifrid (Harris).

All had made their profession in Antwerp, except, of course, the novice, Sister Mary of St. Joseph (Vaughan), and even she had been accepted for the order by Mother Anne of the Ascension. Her father, Richard Vaughan of Courtfield, Monmouthshire, at first opposed his daughter's wish to become a Carmelite, but eventually yielded. Mary was still so young when she presented herself at the English Carmel, that Mother Anne, recognizing that she had a true vocation, sent her to live for a time with a devout lady in Antwerp, who taught her Flemish. She received the habit in the spring of 1648, and was the first to be professed at Lierre, making her vows there on May 27th, 1649, at the age of seventeen.

Sister Mary of St. Joseph lived the life of a saint. Nothing came amiss to her : prayer, weeding the garden, folding linen, all occupations alike found her ever sensibly in God's presence. Although she had been Sub-prioress for six years, no work was too humble for her. Whatever it might be she devoted herself to it to the utmost of her capacity.

' Up to her last illness (says the Necrology of Lierre), she had the task of making the *alpargates*, which, all who know by experience admit, is a very troublesome thing to do. But Sister Mary liked it, esteeming it an honour to be so employed in the service of others. She became so skilful at this work that she did as much as would have kept the hands of three Sisters busy.'

Many a time the Sisters saw Sister Mary's face while she was at prayer suffused with tears, but if one of them ventured a remark about it, she would reply : ' God knows what a poor creature I am and therefore He allows me these sensible feelings, because I am not worthy to be led by the way of the Cross and suffering.' Nevertheless, six months before her death God gave what was looked upon by her Sisters as an outward sign of her interior sanctity.

' As often as any of the community met her (the Necrology relates), they perceived a strange sweet perfume. This also was perceptible during her last illness, and after her death the same fragrance proceeded from the chair she had occupied in the Choir. A head-piece also that she had worn gave off this sweet scent.'

Sister Mary of St. Joseph died peacefully on March 3rd, 1709, in the seventy-ninth year of her age.

Of the other eight nuns Mother Margaret of St. Teresa (Downes) was elected Prioress. As she had been for many years Novice Mistress in Hopland, she had trained nearly all her community. Sister Catherine of the Blessed Sacrament (Windoe), elected Sub-prioress, had entered the Hopland Carmel when she was only thirteen. She esteemed it a great favour to be among those chosen for the foundation in Lierre, where she edified all by her devotedness and humility. She often related that Mother Anne of the Ascension had always taught her ' that it was an imperfection to speak or even remember that one had ever been employed in such or such an office, but that a Carmelite ought to esteem highly the years and time in which she had kept her cell and followed the community.' She had a great love for all her Sisters, and rejoiced in their talents. ' Though I know I am a foolish person myself (she used to say), I cannot but love and esteem those that have wit and employ it well.' Sister Catherine had a tender devotion to the Mother of God, and died on September 27th, 1666, with her eyes fixed ' upon a picture of Our Lady with the Sacred Infant in her arms.'

Sister Eugenia of Jesus was the first to die in Lierre. She had a merry disposition and looked foward to death so eagerly that her Superior forbade her to speak of it. Mother Anne of the Ascension received her in 1634, but she became very ill and was sent back to England. Six years later she re-turned to the English Carmel and made her vows on

August 10th, 1641. She suffered much, both physic-
ally and spiritually, and gladly gave up her soul to
God on August 18th, 1652. Sister Hieronima of
St. Michael followed her to Heaven on September
27th, 1653, but these gaps in the Community were
soon filled by young Sisters of equal fervour, so that
Lierre, like Hopland, became renowned for the
sanctity of its inmates.

Soon after the nuns were settled in *Nazareth*,
Sister Margaret of Jesus had a severe illness, and as
there was very little convenience there for nursing
an invalid, the community in Antwerp tried their
best to persuade her to return to Hopland to be
nursed. This distressed her very much : ' Why
do our dear Sisters regard so poor a creature ?
(she urged). If I die, it imports little where. Nothing grieves me but the trouble I give. I hope for
Our dear Lord's sake that you will have patience
with me, and then I can affirm that all sufferings
are a pleasure to me.' This was more than enough.
The Sisters at Lierre nursed her devotedly during
many weeks of continual fever, and through Our
Lady's intercession she recovered, in spite of being
given up by the doctors. Shortly after this she was
named Mistress of Novices, always an office of great
responsibility, which in the Lierre Carmel involved
special difficulties, for it was just at that time that
Nazareth was beset by devils, who not only created
disturbances, but sometimes attacked Sister Margaret of Jesus in visible form. For some time the
nuns had no rest night or day, so that Mother Lucy
of St. Ignatius (Bedingfeld), who, being elected
Prioress of the English Carmel, Antwerp, on the
death of Mother Teresa of Jesus, passed through

Lierre on her way from Düsseldorf, could not get any sleep on account of the terrible noises that were going on. The next morning she told Mother Margaret of St. Teresa that she wondered how her community could live in such a place, and recommended her to take extra care of the nuns lest they should all fall sick. What distressed the young Novice-mistress most was the effect these diabolic manifestations might have on her novices. One day when she was praying earnestly about this, Our Blessed Lady appeared and assured her that she had each novice under her special protection. Our Lady further ' ordered her to bring their beads, to which she would give a particular blessing, of which each one would be sensible : if they only wore these beads about their necks at night they should find solace and feel the effects of her assistance.' This they truly ever after experienced till their troubles were ended.

After this the devil redoubled his fury against Sister Margaret. The Lierre Chronicle says :

' He (the devil) would sometimes beat her to such a degree as to leave marks and bruises on her body. At other times he would throw her downstairs, and when she was in the garret or other offices alone, the doors of a sudden would be fastened, and the place filled with a horrid darkness, like to a thick smoke or black cloud so that she could not see where she was. In this frightful situation the devil would trail her about for a long time together, till she could scarce any longer fetch her breath or recover so

much strength as to call upon the sacred Names
of Jesus and Mary or make the sign of the
Cross.'

In many other ways did the devil torment her,
sometimes representing that she had deceived herself about Our Lady blessing the beads, until the
Mother of God again appeared to her, and laying her
hand on Sister Margaret's head, asked : ' My
child, why are thou afraid ? May I not bestow my
favours as I please ? ' Then, taking the young
Novice-mistress's beads, she put them into the hand
of the Divine Infant whom she carried on her arm,
and He took them and blessed them, after which
Our Lady gave them back to her, telling her that
as often as she used them she would be comforted.
Our Lady added :

' I have not only blessed those beads, but I am
ready to do the same to any others, if thou askest
this with humility and confidence. For thou
must know, my child, that I have many other
blessings in store for thee. If notwithstanding
this, the devil still continues to tempt thee, know
that it is for thy greater good and his confusion,
and by leaving thee in these uncertainties regarding my favours, I do thee a greater favour than
by giving thee a further assurance, which thou
shalt only receive from thy confessor. This will
keep thee both humble and obedient, and be a
torment and confusion to the devil, for to him
it is worse than hell to have leave and power to
tempt thee, and yet find himself unable once in a
thousand times to effect anything. The worst he
can do is to vex and trouble thee when thou art

unfaithful or disobedient. His power shall be
no more, because my honour is concerned in
making thee happy. Therefore, if thou art
victorious, thou wilt know that it is owing to
me, not to thyself, so thou needst not apprehend
that thy confessor should think thee a saint.
He knows sufficiently thy misery, and my charity
who am the MOTHER OF MERCY.'

This miraculous rosary is carefully and reverently
kept by the Carmelites of Darlington. The beads
seem to possess a miraculous power over evil spirits,
a power still transmitted to any rosary that has
touched the one thus marvellously blessed for Sister
Margaret of Jesus so long ago.

After some delay Mother Margaret of St. Teresa
was able to purchase several 'small straggling'
houses, which she converted into a convent, such as
St. Teresa desired her Carmels to be. From her
first coming to Lierre Sister Margaret had felt certain that these houses, poor and inconvenient as
they were, would one day be their convent, but
when they were purchased by Mother Margaret of
St. Teresa the latter had not intended this. The
alterations were not completed for over a year, but
by then everything was so well contrived that there
was no question of again removing elsewhere.

During the August of 1651 the Prioress, taking
Sister Margaret as her companion, went from
Nazareth to take possession of their new property,
where they had a terrifying experience.

' They had scarce entered the room which was
afterwards the Chapter House (say the Annals)

but there arose on a sudden a violent storm of wind and thunder which filled the place where they stood with a most horrid stench of brimstone. This storm lasted a considerable time, and raised so much dust in the streets that they were scarce passable. In many places barrels and many other things were blown up into the air, which caused great confusion and fear, all affirming that they had never seen the like before, nor could they conceive how the weather, which was fine and settled, should so suddenly change.'

Meanwhile, the community at *Nazareth* were experiencing a somewhat similar trial. The smell of brimstone there was so strong that the nuns felt themselves almost suffocated. It happened that Father Bedingfeld had gone to Antwerp to obtain the bishop's leave for the nuns' removal to their new house. The storm was at its height when he returned to Lierre, and seeing in it something more than natural, he made his way to *Nazareth* without delay, to the great relief of the nuns, one of whom wrote later :

'Here, finding all in disorder, and so much smoke and dust that we were scarce able to see one another, he called for holy water, and said St. John's Gospel, and then sent for an image of Our Lady which was held in great esteem in the house. Sister Ursula, who ran for it, was thrown downstairs by the force of the wind, and the statue dashed against the pavement in the middle of the court, yet neither the Sister nor the image, which was small and curiously carved,

ELIZABETH MOSTYN AS SHE WAS IN 1644
(From a portrait preserved at Carmel House, Darlington.)

Facing page 46

were the least hurt, nor were the crown and
sceptre, which were loose, removed from their
places, to the great astonishment of all, who
expected to find it broken in many pieces. The
statue was then carried to the choir where, with
much ado, a blessed candle being lit, the confessor
began the Litany of Our Lady, during which the
storm seemed to abate, and by the time all was
ended the air reassumed its former calmness and
serenity.'

When Mother Margaret of St. Teresa and her
companion returned, these mysterious happenings
were fully discussed, and the nuns came to the
conclusion that the strange storm had been raised
by the devil, from whose ' tyranny Almighty God
had now finally freed them.'

On the morning after the strange storm, Mother
Margaret of St. Teresa took about seven of the nuns
to their new convent, leaving Sister Margaret of
Jesus at *Nazareth* to superintend the packing and
removal of the goods and furniture belonging to
the community, two or three ' of the most courageous ' being left behind to help her. Thus was
satisfactorily completed the foundation begun so
happily in 1648. The English nuns at Antwerp
shared all expenses and gave generously of
their furniture, church ornaments and other
things.

The Archives of Lanherne have an authenticated
copy of a letter of Gaspar Nemins, written on behalf
of the English Carmelites of Antwerp and Lierre,
but it is too long to be quoted here. There are
also entries in the accounts of the Hopland

Carmel for their expenses connected with the latter foundation.

> " Given at the beginning of our
>   foundation at Lier   .   .   1800 florins
> Item, for different things for
>   the accommodation of our
>   Church and Altar   .   .   675   „
>   ―――
>   2475   „
> Item, given to the same Founda-
>   tion of our Capitals in these
>   Counterys the sum of de vig-
>   inte un mille florins, wh. makes   ―――
>   23,475   „

Besides this, all the furniture of both the Church and Convent was divided between the two houses, except the foundation ornaments given by Lady Lovel. There was also an extraordinary expense noted in the account books of the Hopland Carmel that year for habits, linen, breviaries, etc. ; and in addition to all this, an entry ' To Lawyers and Attorneys, and for the Bull from Rome, 1000 florins.'

The Darlington Carmelites cherish the memory of this first happy home in Lierre. After they came to England in 1794 the nuns hoped to return there, for, as one of them wrote :

> ' We remembered the sweets of Sion, the Beauty of Carmel, and the delights of that peaceful solitude where we had tasted in full the advantages of our holy vocation.'

The following lines, written for the bicentenary of the foundation in Lierre kept in 1848, speak for themselves :

'Deep in the heart of fair Brabant it lies,
    A dreamy old-world town ;
Its red-tiled roofs and lance-like spires
    'Mid woods of golden brown.
A swift white river flashes past its feet,
    On to the woodland space,
And its tall trees clasp o'er the narrow street
    Like friends in close embrace.
'Twas here that Carmel's garden bloomed,
And all the Brabant land perfumed
    With saintly odours pure and rare,
    Beneath the Blessed Margaret's care.
Such virtues flourished in its shade,
That people loved the name, and said:
    " Avila lives in youth once more
    Upon the distant Brabant shore." '

E

CHAPTER IV

SUBPRIORESS AND PRIORESS
1651–1679

WHEN the elections were held in 1651, Sister Margaret of Jesus was chosen by the community as their Mother Subprioress. In that capacity she presided over community exercises in the absence of the Prioress and had charge of all that concerned the recitation of the Divine office and its ceremonial, a work after her own heart. Her elevation to a position of authority only increased Mother Margaret's sense of her own unworthiness, and she continued her practice of assisting the Sisters in any work 'that was mean or humbling, as weeding in the garden, carrying wood, or lighting the fires, all of which she did as if she had been fit for no other employs.' A note among her papers shows the lowly opinion she had of herself:

'Truly I am good for nothing but to take up the place of others who would have served His Divine Majesty much better. How is it possible, my dear Jesus, that thou shouldst still have patience with me, unless it were because Thou findest me really a pitiful object of Thy mercies.

May Thy holy Name be ever praised and glorified in me, Thy unworthy and truly useless servant ! '

Mother Margaret's early training had fitted her to rule a household, and she acquitted herself so well as Subprioress that nothing of consequence in the Convent was done without her advice, and in 1654 the community unanimously elected her Prioress. The choice caused her great consternation :

'When his Lordship the Bishop had declared it to the community according to the usual manner, he congratulated with her Reverence on the choice. She was so surprised and alarmed at it that for some time she could not speak, but kneeling down all bathed in tears, with her hands lifted up, she humbly besought his Lordship not to confirm the election, alleging many reasons and want of abilities which rendered her incapable of so important an office. Among other things she pleaded her want of age, not being as yet thirty, at which my Lord smiling said, " Good Mother, trouble not yourself with that. It will do you no more service than all your other reasons, for suppose it be so, I can and do dispense with that, therefore take courage, my dear daughter, and accept patiently of this cross for the honour and love of God. He will help you to bear it, for I am sure His Hand is in your election, and I cannot leave to confirm what the Holy Ghost has done : be confident that He will direct you in all your actions. Why do you weep and afflict yourself, whilst all these good nuns are full of joy? Why do you continue thus to grieve? Truly, I think if I had but your picture it would represent to the life *Mater dolorosa*".'

In spite of the fact that Our Lord had prepared her for this post of responsibility, it was some time before Mother Margaret recovered from this dreadful shock, as she called it. She tried to resign herself to God's will, and reminded Him of the promise He had made when she was named mistress of novices, that He would not permit her soul to receive any injury by it. She was encouraged by a vision of Mother Anne of St. Augustine, who had received her vows in Antwerp. This holy prioress, she understood, had a very high place in Heaven, and ' had suffered no other Purgatory but the time of her Superiority, because it was not only contrary to her inclinations, but she had met with such crosses and trials during it as entirely cancelled all punishment due to her sins.'

During Mother Anne of St. Augustine's term of office Sister Margaret of Jesus, who knew something of her trials and anxieties, often used to greet her with the words, ' Happy are those Superiors who suffer by their office ! ' This thought had comforted the prioress, whose great regard for Sister Margaret made her train both her and Sister Ursula with special care.

After her election as Prioress, Mother Margaret was also consoled by Mother Anne of the Ascension (Worsley), who appeared to her standing beside Our Blessed Lady :

' She assured Mother Margaret of her particular assistance in all she undertook, admonishing her to be punctual in little observances, and to maintain love and charity one towards another. "For (said Mother Anne) I am crowned with more glory for upholding little observances and fraternal charity than for all those other things you esteem so much, which I did for the good of the Order".'

By successive re-elections Mother Margaret remained in office as Prioress for twenty-five years. During that time she had many opportunities of manifesting her characteristic gifts and also of enduring many trials, which brought out her strength of soul. Bishop Ambrose Capello had friendly relations with the English Carmelites of both Hopland and Lierre. His opinion of the nuns of both Convents can be gathered from a letter written in their favour to the Archbishop of Mechlin, on May 7th, 1658 :[1]

'I can assure Your Lordship that in all my diocese I have not any one Convent of nuns in which is greater Regular Observance, Charity and edifying love than in these two, which may serve for a pattern to as many convents as are in the world. And I am, moreover, bold to say that having had in my charge (being companion to the General Government of the Order of Preachers) to the number of about three thousand, Convents of nuns of the same order (I speak of the Government in general), and having visited in person more than 200 convents of nuns, namely of Italy, Rome, Naples, Cologne, Genoa,

---

[1] An authenticated copy is preserved in Lanherne.

and throughout all France, Spain and Flanders, I can speak with truth I have not found any more Religious, more observant of Regular Discipline, more obedient, or with greater Charity ; nor any that might be said to excel or equal these my two convents of Antwerp and Lierre.'

Bishop Capello held Mother Margaret in high esteem and after presiding at one of her re-elections, he once spoke to the community in her absence, saying that in all his life he had never met her equal ; adding, ' So much wisdom combined with so great humility is rare to be found in these our days.' The nuns over whom Mother Margaret ruled put down in writing what they knew of her virtues, especially of her serene humility and patience under trials and contradictions, in particular those brought upon her through good and holy persons. Some of the headings of these MSS. will sufficiently indicate the reverence with which the saintly Prioress was regarded : ' Her humility, self-contempt and love of poverty ; her spirit of suffering and mortification ; her mildness, affability and tenderness towards her neighbour ; her great confidence in God,' and so on through the gamut of religious virtues. It would be impossible to quote these testimonies *in extenso*, a few examples must suffice. Mother Margaret was not changed by her elevation to a position of authority, rather did she take more than ordinary care to preserve her fidelity to the common observance, and in spite of constant ill-health would not accept any dispensation. She showed great deference to her Discreets, doing nothing regarding the government of the house without their advice :

'Though their judgement did sometimes differ from hers, she left her own to follow theirs, in which way of proceeding she always thought things fell out better than they would have if done according to her own way of thinking, thus attributing all the good success of these affairs to their prudence.'

This habit of self-denial grew to be almost a second nature, so that Mother Margaret used to say that she was never less satisfied than when following her own will. If the younger Sisters, through ignorance or haste, omitted to show their Prioress the customary marks of respect, she was troubled because the Subprioress reproved them about it :

' You cannot trouble me more than by taking notice of such trifles (she would say). If you did but know the dislike I have to hear anything of that nature, you would not give me this mortification. How do you think we shall gain Heaven, or become anything like to Our dear Lord and Saviour, if we bear not with contempts, or accidental neglects ? For my part, I assure you I am more covetous of these few occasions of imitating Him, than worldlings are of the greatest honours. For the love of God, dear Mother Subprioress, let us look well to the main point, that observance be well kept up, and let us give the Sisters good example therein. As for these punctilios, God forbid that we should be so sensible of ourselves as to value them.'

On the other hand, she was most careful herself not to give occasion of any trouble to the Sisters,

' often taking round-about ways in order not to disturb the community by passing them,' and if she borrowed some little trifle ' she would be as careful in using it, and as diligent in restoring it ' as though it were something precious or important. In a word, she constantly tried to carry out in every detail Our Lord's words : ' He that will be first among you, shall be your servant.'

Even when, as Prioress, it was Mother Margaret's duty to reprove the Sisters at Chapter, or on other occasions, she did it so gently and humbly that her words left no sting. She often attributed their faults to her own bad example or lack of vigilance. Poverty she regarded as ' the jewel of the religious state,' and when she made the round of the different offices, nothing pleased her better than to find everything in good order, tidily kept and mended, so that, as she would say : ' All places looked like unto little Bethlehem, poor and neat.' As a rule she cut out any new garments that were required in order that nothing might be wasted by an inexperienced hand, but it gave her much greater pleasure to patch or mend. Sometimes the Sisters would tell her that it was mere loss of time to repair garments so greatly worn, but she would reply :

' Have patience, dear Sisters ; our Spouse knows best what is good for us : this is true poverty by which we hope to obtain eternal riches. I thank God I am never in pain or solicitous on this score, and, if it were within my own choice, it should be rather to want than to possess plenty. God forbid that a poor Teresian should ever apprehend want, since it is poverty

that must make us like unto Our beloved Spouse,
Jesus, who is greatly delighted to see us clothed
with His own livery.'

It was from a spirit of poverty that Mother
Margaret made so much account of every moment
of time. She often said that there was nothing nuns
would have more to answer for than loss of time.
She herself was never idle, and many a time she sat
up at night to mend some garment of which she
knew a Sister was in need. Those in charge used to
wonder how their Mother Prioress found time for
all this, but she would answer with a smile : ' Do
you not know that my little Spouse helps me ? '
The Carmelites in Darlington still possess a very
handsome set of elaborately worked vestments,
complete with cope and antependium, which the
Infant Jesus helped Mother Margaret to embroider.
All is as fresh as if lately done, and a large number
of the ' Mostyn pearls,' a family heirloom, are
worked into the design.[1] Yet, at a word from any
of her nuns, she would put aside all she was doing
and ' listen to their wants and grievances with so
much ease and sweetness as though she had not
other affairs on hand,' never putting a Sister off,
or letting her go away unsatisfied. If it happened
accidentally that any Sister had been forgotten, or
left without what she required, Mother Margaret
was really upset, and blamed herself severely. At
recreation she was the gayest of the gay, and as the
different feasts came round, she would compose
songs which the nuns sang in community, help

[1] These vestments were exhibited in Liverpool on the
occasion of the centenary of Catholic Emancipation, 1929.

them to dress the statue of Our Lady or the Infant Jesus (according to the Flemish custom), and devise all kinds of means of adding to the Sisters' pleasure. Some verses composed by Mother Margaret are still sung by the Darlington community, to a quaint old tune, every day in Advent. The verses are a preparation for Christmas and form an invitation to the Divine Infant to be born again in the hearts of His Carmelite Spouses. The first and last stanzas run thus :

> Sweet blessed little Jesus,
> 'Tis Thee alone can please us,
> Why stayest Thou then so long ?
> Lord hasten now Thy coming
> Our hearts do die with longing
>   To be with Thee made one.

> Then, glorious Queen of Heaven,
> Make haste, give us the Given,
>   The Treasure of our hearts.
> Sweet Lady, stay no longer, .
> But make our souls His manger,
>   No creature shall have part !

When any little feast was prepared, Mother Margaret wished everyone to enjoy it. ' There is a time to be mortified,' she would say, ' but on feast days let us take our own choice and simply what we like best because our dear Lord will have it so. By a good intention the partaking of feast-day fare can be as meritorious as penance and mortification are on other occasions.'

If she noticed that a Sister was not as well as usual she would steal up to her cell, make the bed and put everything in order. On those who were seriously indisposed every care was lavished, and more than once it was the Prioress rather than the doctor who first realized that a Sister was not likely to recover. She was most particular that the Last Sacraments should be administered in good time. Sometimes the Sisters would remind her that the doctor still held out hopes of recovery, but she only replied :

'I have reason to know better, believe me, dear Sister. This, our good religious, will die. I cannot, therefore, rest till she has had the Last Sacraments, and so dispose all things with our confessor as to be ready.'

There was never a case in which the Prioress was mistaken, and when the end came, she would say through her tears :

'I was well inspired ! How good is our blessed Lord so to sweeten our loss ; let us return Him most grateful thanks for this favour. I have a particular joy to see that our dear deceased Sister had all the comfort it was in our power to give her, and that she wanted nothing for her spiritual consolation. Let us congratulate with her in her happiness, and strive to imitate her virtues, that we may deserve the same favour from Our Lord when we come to die.'

It was Mother Margaret's custom to prepare a deceased Sister for burial with her own hands, reckoning it a great privilege to render these last services to ' the temple of the Blessed Trinity and the tabernacle of the Blessed Sacrament.' Her reverence in all this excited devotion in those who assisted, and when all was finished she sat down to write an account of the virtues and good works of the departed Sister.

Though naturally of a hasty temper, Mother Margaret overcame herself so thoroughly that she was never known to lose her patience and self-control. In connection with this perpetual struggle with self, she cultivated a particular devotion to St. Francis de Sales. She constantly recommended charity to the Sisters, saying : ' Love one another ; then Our Lord and His Blessed Mother will love you ! ' Her own feeling towards her spiritual daughters was one of sincere and cordial affection :

' If I had to declare on oath which Sister I loved most (she would say), it would be impossible for me to find any difference.'

Her life was spent in loving thoughtfulness for others, and it was well known among the Sisters that their Prioress would rather suffer in Purgatory for having treated them with too much mildness, than hurt them by harshness or neglect. Now and again she was reproached for showing over great care of the nuns, but she invariably answered :

' It is my duty to serve the spouses of my Infant Spouse. He will have it so. I must not let them want for anything, because, having left all for Him, they have no longer any care of themselves.'

Her kindness to outsiders was equally great. Even when the Convent funds were exceptionally low, no one in need was ever turned away, and Mother Margaret took great pleasure in serving the poor herself. If some of the Sisters remonstrated with her for giving away more than the community could afford, she had an answer ready :

' Hitherto we have had more than was necessary, therefore let us not complain. I trust Our Blessed Lord and His dear Mother to supply our wants, since I am sure they are well pleased and will bless this house for the charity we exercise towards the poor. Our Lord is pleased to style Himself " Father of the Poor," and has promised a reward to all who relieve or assist them in His Name.'

That the saintly Carmelite's trust was abundantly rewarded is proved over and over again in the pages of her Life. Here is one example :

' Whilst His Majesty King Charles II was in exile in these parts, a great part of a regiment of his was quartered in this town, amongst whom were many distressed gentlemen, almost famished for want, having nothing to support themselves withal but the charity of some good people which was inconsiderable, the town being poor and not able to redress their misery, which was such as rendered them real objects of pity. Her Reverence was so moved at it that it caused her many tears of compassion. As long as there was a piece of bread in the house (she said), it was not possible for her to deny it them. Therefore after she had earnestly recommended the affair to the little Infant and His Blessed Mother, she ordered the portress to deny none relief as long as there was anything in the house. She also ordered beef and other meat[1] to be bought for them, which she would sometimes dress and cook her own self, and she was always careful to see it good and in abundance.

For the space of some months there were about twenty persons dined every day in the servants' quarters. Besides diet, she gave constantly to four others, who were Catholics, firing, candles and other necessaries. She also provided the sick with medicines, and paid the doctors for visiting them. The common soldiers were provided with bread and beer, and came in such numbers that the *tourières* [out-sisters] said it was as much as they could do to serve them, so they could scarce find time to say their Office.

This lasted the whole winter, which was sharper than usual, and thereby increased their admiration, for they were then a full community, and were served in the same plentiful manner as usual. Yet their ordinary provisions of firing, corn and beer held out in the same quantity, as if no other had made use of it but their own household, which they could not attribute to anything less than a miracle.

Her Reverence was no less astonished than others at so extraordinary a fact, and doubted not that the Hand of God had been in it, which greatly confirmed her in her hope and confidence in His Divine Providence.'

The same trustful spirit animated Mother Margaret

[1] The eating of flesh meat is forbidden by the Carmelite Rule.

when there was question of receiving a promising subject who could bring no dowry. To the doubts of those who had the right to advise her, she would reply : ' Let us only trust in the Sacred Infant and His Blessed Mother, and we cannot fear want. My Infant Spouse has promised me He will take care of our concerns Himself : be not solicitous on this score.' The relations between this holy nun and her Infant Spouse were of the sweetest, and her own sister, who was for many years her Subprioress, wrote the following charming story after Mother Margaret's death :

' I remember once, in the time of the war, her Reverence used to lay her small provision of money in a basket over her bed's head. Being to pay a considerable sum for certain provisions, and much falling short of money, she called Sister Teresa of St. Augustine[1] and bid her fetch more, but the Sister staying something long, our Mother went herself. The Sister met her, saying : " There was none there " ; but her Reverence, not satisfied, took the basket down again, saying : " I am sure my little Spouse will not serve me so," and taking her little Jesus in her hand (a small wax figure of the Sacred Infant which Mother Margaret always kept with her money), she found underneath a bag of money. At this Sister Teresa was amazed and also those that saw her, only a moment before, take all out of the basket, where she affirmed there was no such bag that she could find. " Nor I neither," said her Reverence, " my Infant Spouse has

[1] Elizabeth Foster (Suffolk) professed June 11th, 1652.

brought it." She found not only sufficient to
make up the sum wanting, but there was left a
quantity for the present use of the house, at which
her Reverence, much transported with joy, said :
" See, Sisters, how good is our little Jesus, not
only to supply us with what is necessary, but He
will always have something in store for His
spouses. Oh, let us confide and put our trust
in Him, who hath never yet failed us." '

The little waxen image of the Infant Jesus is still
treasured in Darlington, and kept as a relic on account
of its connection with the above miracle. It is also the
custom in that Carmel to place a small statue of the
Divine Infant with the money kept in the house,
in imitation of what was done by Mother Margaret.

Another instance of the Prioress's strong faith
and trust occurred in relation to Father Bedingfeld.
He, knowing that the Convent was short of ready
money, begged Mother Margaret to make use of
£100 of his own income, which was in her custody.

To this generous offer, she only replied : ' This will
help us when we are in great distress ; just now our
Spouse must look to it.' After her death, six or
seven years later, the money was found untouched,
with a note that it belonged to the chaplain, together
with a ' good provision ' of coin for immediate use
which no one could account for.

Mother Margaret's childlike trust was not confined
to temporal things, but extended to spiritual matters
whether in regard to this life or the next. In her
many trials her faith never wavered ; ' God knows
best what is good for us,' were the words ever in
her heart and on her lips. It was the offence against

God, rather than her own suffering, that afflicted her most. When religious persecution broke out again in England after the infamous *Popish Plot*, the news made a deep impression upon her. After some moments of silence, she exclaimed :

'If these good men did only suffer, it were little, or rather glorious, since they die for their faith. But how many souls in that poor Kingdom will run the hazard of being lost for ever !

Dear Sisters, for the love of God, let us employ all our force that His Divine Goodness may vouchsafe to cast a merciful eye on our friends and country. Let us implore the help and mediation of our most tender Mother, the blessed Virgin Mary.'

Perhaps the greatest trials of Mother Margaret's life arose from calumny and detraction. Canon Bedingfeld, in writing of this cross, quotes a passage from St. Bernard : 'Persons the most perfect are still wanting in something towards an accomplished sanctity unless their reputation be also slandered ; for until then they cannot be said to be in all conformable to Jesus Christ.'

Mother Margaret's sensitive nature suffered intensely when those she had trusted abused her confidence, or misrepresented her actions and intentions.

'In what regarded her own particular (writes Canon Bedingfeld) she was condemned as a hypocrite, and one that loved changes ; her pretended zeal of perfection was nothing but an effect of pride ; she was deluded by the devil, and

F

gave just reason to apprehend the state of her soul and many things of a like nature. What touched her to the quick was that many things regarding her conscience, interior graces, and favours communicated to her soul were divulged and made public, not only to several of our English convents, but even as far as England. She became the talk and ridicule of certain devotees, for all who heard of her took the liberty to condemn her conduct and to deride her manner of prayer. Many, even pious persons, proceeded so far as to reprehend her in their letters, saying she wanted experience, and that her proceedings would soon spoil this new convent, and reduce to nothing the spirit of St. Teresa, to the great discredit of the Order. They would also, by a feigned compassion, bewail the misfortunes of the poor nuns who, they doubted not, were put to great sufferings and inconveniences by her unsettled way of government.'

The holy Prioress bore all this with uncomplaining patience, and refused to defend herself, even going out of her way to show respect and affection for those who were endeavouring to cast discredit upon her. This was especially the case with the one or two within the community who, on account of these false reports, lost their confidence for a time, and met her advances with coldness and ingratitude.

That the above accusations were due to prejudice and pre-conceived ideas is remarkably shown by what happened to a very holy man who, for a time, was bitterly opposed to Mother Margaret. One day, when passing through Lierre, this priest felt moved to call at the English Carmel. Mother Margaret received him very graciously, thanking him for many favours he had formerly done her. This generosity so worked upon his better feelings that he fell upon his knees and begged pardon for 'the many unreasonable troubles' he had caused her. Filled with confusion, the holy Prioress replied :

'Our blessed Lady and her Infant Son have permitted this and much more from others for my greater good. Perhaps I should have been a lost soul had it happened otherways ; you know my sins and wicked life deserve much more than all that has been said about me. I beseech you to believe this truth. I have never yet repined at, nor thought the worse of those who blamed me, though I could not but know I was innocent of many things laid to my charge. Since I was not ignorant but very sensible of my faults, I did not wonder the world should have so bad an opinion of me. Did they but know my poverty and imperfections as they are manifest to yourself, they would far exceed all that has been said of me. If it were lawful for me to declare them, I would expose myself to still more grievous censures, that so the mercies of my God might be the more adored and admired by all.'

After this, Mother Margaret opened her heart to her friend, giving him an account, not only of her own soul, but of the happy and flourishing state of her community. At this he was so much edified and

rejoiced that he assured her that she was in the right
way, her conduct being conformable to the Spirit
of God, Who, through further trials, would accomplish all His designs in her to His own glory, and
he spiritual progress and profit of many.

CHAPTER V

DEATH AND REPUTATION OF SANCTITY

1679–1682

DURING the early months of the year 1679 the community in Lierre noticed that their Mother Prioress was pensive and apparently ill-at-ease, as though there was something she thought ought to be done which she could not accomplish. It happened that workmen were in the Convent, so that the enclosure was open, and the nuns feared that some accident had happened which distressed her. Some of the Sisters asked her whether this was the case, but she always reassured them, saying that nothing to do with this world could trouble her, so long as she was sure she was doing 'the Will of her Sweet Infant Jesus!' Nevertheless, she often cast her eyes up to Heaven, and said with a deep sigh : ' O my God, what wilt Thou have me to do ? '

The Subprioress, Mother Ursula, once surprised her in her cell writing, her face inflamed as it was wont to be in prayer, or when she spoke of heavenly things. For a few moments Mother Ursula stood spellbound, but very soon her sister noticed her presence, and laying down her pen, folded up the paper upon which she was writing. There was perfect confidence between the two, and this act on Mother Margaret's part awakened her younger sister's curiosity. She even went as far as asking to see the paper, only to receive the reply : ' It is of no importance; but having little to do I was writing down my thoughts to ease my mind. Our blessed Lord knows best what is good for us. Let us trust Him, and resolve to suffer courageously for His love.'

After Mother Margaret's death this paper was found among her other writings, and it clearly showed that God had warned her that He was soon to call her to Himself. From this time onwards the community noted a change in their beloved Prioress. She grew very weak, and had to force herself to take an interest in what was going on around her. This was so unlike her that the nuns put it down to her suffering state, and she herself, striving not to give way, managed to fulfil all the ordinary duties of community life until August 9th, the vigil of St. Laurence. This great martyr's feast-day was the anniversary of her clothing, and she always kept it as a day of special devotion. For many years the recurrence of this festival had brought her some special cross or suffering, which she looked upon as a sign that St. Laurence had her under his protection, she, on her side, honouring him as her particular patron in suffering.

' Now (says the chronicle) finding herself seized upon by a violent fever, she was forced to go to bed saying : " This is more than ordinarily great ; St. Laurence, help me to bear it, and then God's Holy Will be done." She could get no rest all that night, and the next morning was found so very ill that the doctor was immediately sent for. He thought her in so poor a condition that he would not permit her to rise that day, lest she should endanger herself. This was a great affliction to her as it deprived her of the happiness of Communion after which she eagerly thirsted; yet she passed it over with an amorous complaint saying: " Saint Laurence is now too severe, for there is no suffering so sensible to me as the being deprived of this heavenly food." She continued greatly indisposed all that day, but the day following, the doctor found her without fever and would have ordered physic, only the great heats and her exceeding weakness caused him to defer it.

In the meantime she rose and went to the choir and communicated, though with much difficulty, for she looked like one that had lain a long time sick in bed : her eyes had grown hollow and her whole countenance so changed that it struck with amaze all who beheld her.'

From August 12th to the 24th Mother Margaret dragged herself about, fulfilling all her duties as usual. On the feast of St. Bartholomew she was even able to converse with some visitors, but while she was with them an attack of uncontrollable pain came upon her which she was not able to hide. As she left the Sisters, she looked back at them with such compassion that they all felt it would be the last time she would be there among them. Canon Bedingfeld, who was present, also noticed how ill she looked and persuaded her to go straight to bed. Mother Margaret obeyed, but nothing gave her any relief, and she was again in high fever. The doctor was summoned in haste, but the saintly Prioress already knew that the end was near. She sent for the community, and told 'her dear children with the tenderness of an affectionate mother that her time was come.' For their sakes she accepted whatever remedies were offered her, but it was plain to see that she was not long for this world.

'She bid them take courage, and endeavoured to comfort them with hopes of her life (she was only fifty-three) saying she would do all her part, and was sure nothing would be wanting on theirs. As she was wholly resigned to the Divine Will of God, so she desired them to be, and to leave all to the merciful disposal of her Infant Spouse, Jesus, and His blessed Mother, asking for her only patience in her excessive suffering.'

When the Sisters found that no remedy seemed to give their dearly loved Mother any relief they could not restrain their grief, and her room was filled with their sobs and tears. In spite of the intense pain she was suffering, Mother Margaret thereupon reproached them for praying that her life might be prolonged.

'Why would you deprive me of the happiness I have so long thirsted after? (she said). What is it to live ten or twelve years more? Death must come at last. It is a debt we must all pay to nature before we can come to live eternally. I have lived but too long, except I had made better use of my time.'

She frequently adored and praised God for all His goodness to her, particularly for 'having brought her up a child of His Holy Church in the heart of an heretical country,' and for allowing her to serve Him as a daughter of St. Teresa. Her friend, Fr. William Morgan, S. J. went to the Carmel to see if there was anything he could do for her. She was glad to have a talk with him, but told Mother Ursula that she had no troubles of conscience to settle. Nevertheless, he stayed a considerable time, and Mother Margaret begged his prayers and blessing when he was leaving. This Father Morgan was born in 1624, in Flintshire, where he afterwards worked as a Jesuit missionary, having his headquarters at St. Winifred's Residence, and he had often been of great assistance to the English Carmelites.

On the feast of St. Augustine, Mother Ursula begged Our Lord, after her Communion, to accept her life instead of that of her sister, but when the latter heard this she gently reproached her : 'You know not what you ask (she said). Our Blessed Lady and her sweet Son know best what is good for you and me, and therefore we ought to be entirely resigned to His Divine Will.'

When the doctor came, he found Mother Margaret so much worse that he consented to her having the Last Sacraments, which she had already asked for several times. The news rejoiced her greatly. ' How good is my dear Lord to come to me (she exclaimed), there is nothing I desire more ! ' she told the Sisters waiting upon her, who were all weeping, that she was not worth one tear, and that God could easily supply their want of her, while she

herself would be   to help them much better
from heaven. Sh   ook a tender farewell of each
one, and then departed herself wholly to preparing
for death—

> ' reciting acts of gratitude, love and confidence ;
> expressing her thirsting desires of those happy
> moments wherein she was to partake of her most
> beloved Lord in His most comfortable Sacrament,
> which she received with singular humility and
> sense of devotion, often saying with much fer-
> vour : " Lord, Thou knowest that I love Thee
> above all things, and there is nothing can separate
> me from Thee : nor do I desire anything but the
> accomplishment of Thy blessed Will." '

All that day passed in suffering and prayer, for
Canon Bedingfeld still delayed giving her the Last
Anointing.   Next morning, however, the community assembled and accompanied the confessor
with the Holy Oils to the infirmary.

> ' When they were come in, her Reverence with
> great humility begged pardon of all her offences,
> and said that by the merits of Christ she confi-
> dently hoped for eternal salvation, entreating the
> Sisters to beg it of Our Lord for her.   Then she
> raised herself up, helped to loosen her head-dress,
> and betwixt every unction, joining her hands,
> gave thanks to God for making her a child of
> His Holy Church, desiring and hoping to die a
> true one.   The ceremonies being ended, she
> called for the plenary indulgence of the Order,
> which she received and heard read with great

attention, rendering infinite thanks to her Creator for so many favours.'

After that the community withdrew, except the Subprioress, and the two sisters were alone together for the last time on earth. She gave Mother Ursula messages for her friends, and each member of their family, especially Sir Edward Mostyn, their only surviving brother:

' I had a great desire to see him (she said), for my own comfort and his, but Our Lord would not have it so. When I come to Heaven I shall do them more good, and shall be mindful of our poor family. God give them grace to serve Him well; this shall be my prayer when I shall be so happy as to enjoy my Lord for ever.'

Then taking Mother Ursula's hand in her own, she added:

' Courage, dear sister, do not weep, but rather congratulate with me, for the mercies of my God are infinite; what praises shall I ever be able to give Him for His goodness towards us both! Have patience; sweet Jesus and His blessed Mother will help you to suffer much. Do not think I leave you because it is their pleasure we must part in this life; be assured my care shall be more than ever for you, and all that concerns you, in a more efficacious manner than if I were to remain with you. Put your confidence, there-fore, in Jesus and Mary, and give all the interest you have in me into their hands, who know best what is good for us both. What I desire at present is that you will not leave me this night before you have closed my eyes.'

About nine o'clock that evening the doctor came again to see Mother Margaret, accompanied by Canon Bedingfeld and his eldest brother, Sir Henry, who was a great benefactor of the Carmel in Lierre. Whilst the doctor was feeling her pulse the dying Prioress smiled at him, saying : ' There is now no more to be done,' and regretting that she had nothing but her prayers with which to repay his care. Then she turned to Sir Henry Bedingfeld and thanked him for all he had done for the house. She was still her unselfish self, for when the Canon offered to stay with her through the night she replied that as he was not well she feared it might do him harm, otherwise it would be a great comfort to her. Her one wish was to receive Holy Viaticum again before she died, and Canon Bedingfeld said he would bring the Blessed Sacrament if she could wait till midnight. ' God be praised (was her answer) ; that will not be long for it is eleven now.'

Soon after this she collapsed through great weakness and asked for something to refresh her ; then, still fully conscious, counted the quarters till twelve o'clock struck. The story of her last hours is lovingly told in the MS. life :

' As soon as she beheld our dear Lord, whom she so affectionately loved, her whole countenance changed and became adorned with a venerable aspect whilst, with her hands fixed together, she uttered most moving and amorous expressions to her beloved Spouse, Whom she received with great devotion, and then remained silent a considerable time. Canon Bedingfeld came again, and kneeling close by her, suggested divers acts of love to God and confidence in His mercies, which her Reverence repeated with so great fervour that he was moved to tears and humbly begged her prayers for himself and all present, saying he would also pray for her all the days of his life. At this she bowed her head, and replied : " God reward your Reverence, I could not wish a greater favour." Then, at his request, she gave her blessing to her afflicted dear children, desiring them not to grieve but to pray for her. " Be but obedient in all to your Superiors, (said she), and carefully observe your holy Rule and Constitutions, and nothing will ever be wanting to you. Endeavour particularly to conserve and increase that charity and union you have always had amongst you and, believe me, our blessed Lady and her sweet Son will defend, nourish and be ever in the midst of you. Let each one take these points seriously to heart, and beware of the least defect in them. It is these, above all, which will increase perfection in your souls, and uphold this house. To love one another, dear Sisters, you know is Our Lord's commandment. Regard not, I beseech you, my ill example, faults and negligences, for which I humbly beg pardon of you all, and for everything wherein I may have offended you ! "

Then she took leave of each one in a most cordial manner, hoping to see them all again with her in heaven. After this, raising herself on her pillow, she said : " Although I find myself in my agony, yet methinks I can better stir and help myself than I have been able to do all the time of my sickness ; neither am I sensible of much pain!" Then beckoning to Mother Subprioress to draw near, she spoke to her in a low voice as follows : "My dear sister, now approaches the happy time of my departure out of this miserable world in which you have yet much to suffer ; but Our Lord will help you to carry your cross, and assist you with His grace to perform His Will in all. Whether it be agreeable or disagreeable it imports little, so we be but faithful to God, and bear with patience what He sends. I desire you, for the love of God and all the affection there has been between us, let me be buried in the poorest habit in the house, and see you do not permit the Sisters to say anything in my praise, but pray for me, your dear sister."

At this the Subprioress, all in tears, begged of her Reverence that she would obtain for her the favour quickly to follow her, but she replied : "Leave that to God, and desire nothing but His blessed Will. You may be confident, my care of you shall be the same, and when I am so happy as to come to heaven, if I have power there, you shall partake of it in that manner as shall be most to your comfort and advantage. Be sure you rely on and obey our good confessor in all. He is a true friend and will help you. Take courage, therefore, the Sisters all love you most dearly." Then, naming some of the community, she added: "These are very discreet and virtuous, they will assist you. Have confidence in them and endeavour to uphold observance and charity in the community." After this her Reverence asked what o'clock it was, and Mother Subprioress answered : "A little past four." "Is it no more ? " she said, and began to count: " five, six, seven ! " which was the time she departed and we may suppose known to her, since she added : " My dear Jesus, when and as Thou pleasest." After raising and bowing her head to the community with a cheerful countenance, as though she was taking her last farewell, she fixed her eyes on a picture of our blessed Lady with the Infant Jesus in her arms[1] for a considerable time, which made all think the hour of her departure was near at hand.

The confessor therefore began the Litany and Recommendation of the Soul, to which her Reverence answered in so calm and reverent a manner that all could hear her. But Canon Bedingfeld, fearing she would spend herself thereby, said : " Good Mother, do not force yourself ; it is sufficient you answer with your heart." This gave her an occasion of practising, even in her death, her choice virtue of obedience, for she immediately bowed to him and ceased to answer. Her countenance after this becoming more than ordinarily cheerful, as one not able to express her joy, he supposed she saw something particular, and remembering the promise our blessed Lady had formerly made to her of visibly assisting her at death, he was moved to ask her if our blessed Lady was not there, to which she replied : " Oh yes, dear sir ; our blessed Lady, St. Francis de Sales, my great St. Austin, the humble St. Francis, St. Bernard and all the Court

---

[1] This picture is still in the possession of the Community in Darlington. It is always brought to the Sisters when they are dying.

of H⸻ After this, with a most sweet
cou⸻, she instantly rendered her most
happy soul into the hands of her Creator, on
August 29th, at seven in the morning, in the
year of Our Lord 1679.'

After death Mother Margaret of Jesus looked as
peaceful and serene as she had done during life.
According to custom her body, clothed in the
Carmelite habit, lay exposed in the nuns' choir
until the day of the funeral. There was such an
atmosphere of sweetness and sanctity about her
that all who prayed beside her were moved to
devotion and respect. Her burial was carried out
with all the solemnity the house could afford, a
High Mass of Requiem being offered for the repose
of her soul. This was attended by a great concourse
of people from all parts of Lierre, who regarded the
deceased Prioress as a saint. Many begged for a
piece of her habit, or of anything else she had used,
which they carefully kept as relics. For many
years her memory was revered, and people in
trouble had recourse to her intercession, coming
to the nuns' church with votive candles to be burnt
for their intentions. Their faith was often rewarded,
and they returned to offer thanksgiving for favours
received, more convinced than ever that Mother
Margaret was a saint.

The community over which she had ruled for
close on a quarter of a century shared the opinion
of the good people of Lierre, but in recording their
experiences they took care to add : ' We cannot
forbear saying with the people Mother Margaret is a
true saint, but we conform ourselves in all to the

submission which is due to higher powers.' Having taken this precaution they relate a wonderful cure that took place in the convent itself.

About five months after the holy Prioress's death, Anna Maria of St. Joseph, a young lay-sister, ' very handy and serviceable to the community,' fell sick of a violent fever. For six days she ran a high temperature and was brought to death's door, so that the doctor advised the administration of the Last Sacraments. When the ceremonies were over, the fever grew much worse, and two Sisters were left to watch by her during the night. While they were with her, she looked so dreadfully ill that they thought she was in her last agony, and one of them proposed calling the community. But the invalid immediately began to tell them of a great light she had seen, upon which, imagining she was delirious, they drew the bed-curtains together, still intending to call the nuns. However the sick Sister lay quite still and was breathing quietly. She remained like this till after the Conventual Mass, and then asked to see the confessor. Canon Bedingfeld went to her at once, and she told him the following wonderful story:

' Seeing death so near, I was seized with a great terror and apprehension of it, finding myself but very ill-prepared for eternity. Therefore, having great confidence in dear Mother Margaret, who was best acquainted, after God, with the poverty of my soul, I made a most humble and earnest petition to her that she would intercede to our blessed Lord for my recovery, to the end I might mend my life and serve Him better. My prayer was no sooner ended, but I thought I saw this

G

dear Mother in the chamber and a glorious light
about the bed, which revived and comforted me
above measure, so that I found myself much at
ease till the time of Mass. During Mass I redoubled my prayer with greater confidence and
devotion than before, when on a sudden there
appeared a heavenly light, and our venerable
Mother bearing the Divine Jesus in her arms upon
a white cloth, with straw underneath, some of
the ears of which hung lower than the cloth.
Her black veil glittered as if it were full of stars,
but she had her own countenance, though glorious,
and said to me : " My child, your hour of death
was come ; but since out of your desire of living
to serve God more perfectly you have put your
confidence in me, I have obtained health for you."
In that very moment I found myself perfectly
well.'

The narrative goes on to say that Sister Anna
Maria would have got up at once and gone about
her work, had she not been told to remain in bed
in order to have the doctor's approbation of her
cure. When, in the course of the morning, the
doctor arrived he was greatly surprised at so sudden
and complete a recovery, declaring it to be above
the work of nature. He thoroughly examined his
patient, but found no reason for keeping her in
bed. The next morning she went to Mass and
Holy Communion with the rest of the community,
and was ready to go to her work as usual. ' This
happened (says the chronicle) on January 10th in
the year of Our Lord 1680, the account being signed
in form by the doctor, confessor, prioress and

discreets.' Nor was the community, as a whole,
left without manifest tokens that their beloved
Prioress was mindful of them in heaven. Canon
Bedingfeld assured the Sisters that Mother Margaret
was often amongst them. She made her presence
known to individual Sisters 'by an odoriferous
and heavenly fragrancy which they found about
them.' On August 12th, 1680, the first anniversary
of her profession since her holy death the previous
year, the whole Convent was filled with a like
fragrance, which was perceptible to all. The
perfume which filled the whole Convent came with
great strength from the vault where Mother
Margaret's body lay, making itself felt from the
First Vespers of the Feast of St. Clare, and persisting
till the conclusion of the Second Vespers on the
following day. It aroused unusual devotion and
joy in all who perceived it, and this heavenly favour
was repeated for the same length of time and in the
same manner on the day of her first anniversary, the
Feast of the Beheading of St. John the Baptist. All
the nuns were animated by this supernatural
experience ' to new zeal and fervour in the perform-
ance of their religious duties,' and encouraged to
make fresh efforts to imitate the many virtues they
had admired in their saintly Mother.

Sir Edward Mostyn also had a strange experience
with regard to his well-beloved sister, whose portrait
in her religious habit he always kept on the wall,
by his bedside. Of this portrait Mother Ursula
related the following coincidence :

' The same night that her Reverence died, her
brother was awoke out of his sleep by a great

noise in his chamber, but could not imagine what caused it, for he was much altered and could not rest after. On rising in the morning he found the picture taken down, and set on the other side of the room over against the door, and all who came in must see it. To his thinking it seemed to cast a more resplendent sweetness than ordinary, at which he was much amazed and called several in the house, who observed the same change in the picture. All said it looked heavenly, but could not tell what judgement to make of it, not dreaming of her death, for this being in England they had not so much as heard of her being sick; but it happened the same night as she died, as we understood after.'

About two and a half years after Mother Margaret's death Lierre lost another holy and beloved nun, Mother Margaret of St. Teresa. When the dead-cellar was opened for her burial a remarkable prodigy was discovered regarding the deceased Prioress. The previous winter serious floods occurred which had filled the cellar with water, and the account given of the opening of the vault begins by stating this :

' It could not be other ways expected, but the mud and dirty water must needs naturally speaking make an unsavoury smell and cause much filth, but on the contrary, when the vault was opened it rather smelt sweet and wholesome, to the great admiration and astonishment of the workmen that opened the door. All the sign that there had been water in it was that all the coffins were wet and mouldy, like soaked in water. Only our dear Mother's was as dry and fresh as if it had stood in some closet, so that we may piously imagine that her pure and unspotted body even preserved the chest that enclosed it.

'Of this several persons of quality were eye-witnesses, for the inclosure also at that time happened to be open. Her own brother, Sir Edward Mostyn, was one. We did expect him here before in her lifetime, but he came not till then. He esteemed the dead-cellar a precious reliquary, as also the bed whereon Mother Margaret died, so great a veneration had he for this dear sister, attributing all his prosperity to her prayers.'

Canon Bedingfeld had such a respect and admiration for Mother Margaret that he wrote a circular letter to announce her death to the English Carmel in Antwerp, and its daughter convents, of which the autograph is still preserved in Darlington. He calls her ' our dearest Mother Margaret of Jesus,' and, speaking for the nuns in Lierre, says her unexpected death was ' the most heavy cross that ever befell us.' After giving various instances of her unusual virtue, he adds : ' This is but a touch of what may be said, for really each one virtue considered in her well apart seems to bear the prize.' This praise, coming from Mother Margaret's confidant and spiritual director, is a sufficient testimony to the holiness of her life.

Once, when Mother Margaret was still in Antwerp, Father Andrew White, S.J., told her that she would one day go to England. This prophecy is considered to be verified by her holy remains having been brought over to this country in 1794. When the community made its hurried flight from Lierre, Mother Mary Anne Bernard Housman, the Prioress, with two other Sisters, without any remembrance of the prophecy, hurried down to the dead-cellar, and secured the venerated remains of both Mothers Margaret of Jesus and Ursula of All Saints, which they brought over to England, and which are still kept with reverent care in Carmel House, Darlington.

By unanimous election Mother Ursula succeeded her sister as Prioress, and was continued in office for twenty-two years. She died in the odour of sanctity on March 19th, 1700, aged seventy-four. Three daughters of Sir Edward Mostyn also became Carmelites in Lierre : the eldest, Elizabeth, was professed as Lucy of the Holy Ghost in 1670, the youngest, Anne, became in religion Mary Anne of St. Winifred. The second girl, Margaret, once called at Lierre to see her aunts, and Mother Margaret of Jesus told her that she would end her days as a Carmelite in that Convent. The younger Margaret, a gay high-spirited girl, replied that she would take good care not to do that, and accordingly married a gentleman living in Oxfordshire, who was a widower. For some years her life was happy enough, but after her husband's death she determined to be a nun, though not in Lierre. She went first to the Poor Clares in Rouen, then to the Benedictines in Dunkirk, but could not settle in either place, for God wanted her to be a Carmelite. At last grace conquered. She was received by Mother Ursula in 1693, and became a cheerful and useful member of the community, being known as

Margaret Teresa of the Immaculate Conception. Three years after her aunt's death, she was elected Prioress, and held that position till her death in February, 1743 (New Style). Thus it came about that, for over three-quarters of the first century of its existence, the Carmel in Lierre was ruled by members of the Mostyn family. No wonder their memory is held in benediction and that their example will ever be a living force in the Darlington community.

In fact, just over one hundred years later, Mother Margaret of Jesus sent (so to speak) another member of her family to become a daughter of St. Teresa in the Carmel she had loved so well. In 1850, Anna Maria Bunbury, then twenty-one, who from her childhood had desired to belong to Our Lady, was, by a special dispensation, allowed to spend one month within the enclosure at Carmel House, before entering as a postulant. This unusual privilege was asked for by her mother, who, after refusing consent to allow Anna Maria to enter earlier, hoped by this means to dissuade her from her purpose. Naturally enough the expedient had just the opposite effect, and on December 7th of the same year Anna received the Carmelite habit, and was professed on February 19th, 1852 as Mary Teresa of the Protection of Our Blessed Lady. The last part of her name was taken in thanksgiving for a sudden cure of some affection of the throat which took place during her stay as a visitor in Carmel House.

After the month there, she returned home taking with her the life of Mother Margaret Mostyn (then only in MS.) which she had read with great devotion, and wished to show to Lady Mostyn of Talacre

whom she knew well.   Lady Mostyn (*née* Slaughter),
who knew nothing of her husband's holy collateral
ancestress, sent the MSS. to the Franciscan Convent
at Taunton, where her youngest daughter, Catherine,
was at school, begging that 'Kitty' might be allowed
to read it.   The request was granted, but with the
caution that, ' it was not to be shown to her school-
fellows.'

When Sister Mary Teresa was elected Prioress of
Carmel House in 1876, she interested Father H. J.
Coleridge, S.J., in Mother Margaret's life, and he
went through the relevant MSS. preserved in the
nuns' archives, and published the book as a volume
in the *Quarterly Series* under the title of *Mother
Margaret Mostyn* (Burns and Oates, Portman Street,
London, 1878).

Meanwhile Kitty Mostyn developed a great
devotion to Mother Margaret and made up her
mind to follow in her footsteps.   During the Lent
of 1860 she left home early one morning because
she could not bear to say good-bye to her beloved
mother, and was clothed on May 29th.   In memory
of her saintly ancestors she took the name Margaret
Ursula of the Infant Jesus, and was professed on
May 30th, 1861.   Lady Mostyn made many handsome gifts to the community, and among them two
beautiful oak shrines for the ' relics ' of Mothers
Margaret of Jesus and Ursula of All Saints.   Up to
that time these precious remains had been kept in
the wooden box in which they had been brought
from Lierre, but with the Bishop's permission they
were encased in the new shrines, which now stand
on either side of the grate in the nuns' choir.
' Kitty ' was allowed to be present at the ceremony,

and eagerly watched the opening of the box. On beholding two skulls, she burst into tears in sheer disappointment. 'Of course (she said in answer to her Mistress of Novices, Mother Mary Teresa Bunbury) I thought dear Mother Margaret was *incorrupt !*' However, she recovered from her disappointment and as assistant sacristan, 'it was her privilege to place vases of flowers before the shrines on the dear Mothers' clothing and profession days.'

Sister Margaret Ursula filled many offices in succession, one being 'Garden Sister,' which gave her great delight, for she loved flowers. She had a lowly opinion of herself and used to say to the other nuns : '*You* have your prayers and devotions to offer to Our Blessed Lord, but *I* have nothing but my little flowers.' She was always merry at recreation and had a beautiful voice, deep and rich, so that she was playfully called 'The Organ.' After living a hidden and holy life, Sister Margaret Ursula died in her sleep on May 5th, 1917 just as the midday '*Regina*' was ringing. She was eighty years of age, but her heart was always the heart of a child, and the nuns strewed her mantle with primroses and covered with daffodils the bier on which she was borne to her last long rest. R.I.P.

CHAPTER VI

SOME SUPERNATURAL FAVOURS

FATHER H. J. Coleridge, writing for *The Month* in June, 1878, an article entitled *A Carmelite Family*, sketches the story of the five Mostyns who were nuns in Lierre, and shows how the memoirs from which the first life of Mother Margaret of Jesus was compiled throw light upon the customs and training of old Catholic families in England during the days of persecution. He remarked in conclusion :

'It is impossible not to see how much that training had to do with the mature and solid sanctity which characterizes the lives of which we have been speaking. There is not a single instance in which these ladies derived their inspiration to the perfect service of God in the cloister from the urgent advice of a confessor, or from the excitement, or supposed excitement, of a retreat, or even from a sermon. The confessors, so far as we are told of their action, sided with the parents in dissuading the girls from their self-sacrifice, at least as long as there was any chance that they might be mistaken, or any wisdom in putting their resolutions to the test of opposition.

The intense family affection also which distinguishes their lives was an element likely to work rather against the execution of their designs than in favour of it. But we catch glimpses of family habits—the reverence of children for their parents, the daily routine of piety, the constant intercourse with the resident priest, the frequenting of the domestic chapel, the active employment of young girls in household duties, and their training in useful womanly accomplishments. It is of such as they were made of that the human treasures of the Church are formed. Souls such as theirs are capable, when fortified by grace, of the noblest sacrifices that God asks of those whom He draws to Himself, and it is to the prayers of such as they were that we owe it in great measure that there is the Catholic faith and the Catholic Church in the country in which we live.'

It is thanks to Canon Edmund Bedingfeld, who put Mother Margaret of Jesus under obedience to write an account of her supernatural favours, and to the Bishop of Antwerp, who bid the nuns in Lierre to write their recollections concerning her, that some idea can still be formed of how God dealt with at least one of those who gave their all for His love.

From her earliest childhood Margaret had received unusual graces, and she continued to do so all her life. Only a few of those recorded can be mentioned here.

She was often tempted, on account of what she felt of her unworthiness, to abstain from receiving

Holy Communion, and one morning in particular her fears were stronger than usual.

'She remained in a sort of wavering suspense till after the elevation, when she again renewed her resolutions, thinking that if she was to be a lost soul it should be through obedience. In this strife our blessed Lady appeared to her with her Infant Son, who said those acts of obedience had brought them to assist her in preparation and strengthen her against like temptations for the future. As soon as she had received the Sacred Host, in which she saw Our Lord distinctly, He told her He would show her the dignity and benefit of communicating, and how every Communion worthily received would appear in heaven. After this, she saw Our Lord all glorious and bright, or rather all Heaven in Him, and understood that all glorified bodies are made glorious and receive their splendour from His Sacred Humanity ; and as His Sacred Humanity shall shine in every glorified body, so shall every Communion give new lustre to our bodies, so that the more frequently we communicate, and according to the fervour and love with which we dispose ourselves for it, so shall we partake of the glory of the Sacred Humanity, and by this to a proportion of His Divinity, which the soul shall see and enjoy more or less, according to its fidelity in corresponding with the influences of light and graces that have been communicated to it in the Sacrament.

Then Our Lord said to her in a most sweet manner : " Now, my child, I hope thou wilt ever be eager and solicitous to receive Me often, and dispose thyself thereto to the best of thy power since every Communion, as thou seest, and every act of virtue thou dost then exercise shall be so abundantly rewarded ! " '

Our Lord then showed Himself to Mother Margaret as Priest, the glory of which appearance was so great that it caused her to forget all that had gone before. He told her never to be troubled if she had no sensible fervour and devotion when preparing for Holy Communion, nor oppressed with the contrary, for the benefit of receiving the Blessed Sacrament in no way depended upon this : a simple though obscure faith that He is always the same, as great, powerful, good and merciful in the depth of aridity as in the height of consolations will abundantly make up for all other deficiencies. By approaching the Sacraments in these humble sentiments, He said, after having made use of the proper prayers for this purpose although in the greatest dryness and insensibility, the same graces and benefits may be received as when they are performed with the most lively sentiments of devotion, which latter are sometimes more apt to deceive than to sanctify us. Oftentimes a Communion received without any apparent effects of devotion, only because obedience requires it, surpasses any others in which we receive satisfaction, is far more pleasing to God, and will be rewarded with a much greater glory in heaven.

' Never, therefore, be anxious (Our Lord continued) for past sins and imperfections when thou shouldst be preparing thyself to receive

Me; for it is a mere illusion of the devil who, under the specious pretext of a false humility, would dissuade thee from approaching so often to this Sacred Table on account of thy unworthiness; or, if he cannot effect this, to hinder thee at least from that devotion which thou mightest otherwise attain : and, by thus throwing thee into perplexities, he deprives thee of the exercise of those loving and affectionate desires, which he knows to be so pleasing to Me. Thou mayest be assured that it is not what is past that puts an obstacle to My graces, since all that by a simple act of the will is effaced. It is the present disposition the soul is in that renders it fit or unfit for the receiving of this Divine Food, so that a wilful attachment or affection to any venial sin is a greater obstacle than all the other sins of thy past life once repented of; and a disposition to be careless or negligent in little things, however small they may be, is more displeasing to Me, and hinders the effects of grace in thy soul more than if thou didst come to receive Me with divers venial sins with a due sorrow and resolution of amendment.'

Our Lord further assured Mother Margaret that in believing and practising whatever her confessor advised she would be certain of His Will, and that she was not to be discouraged when she fell into some imperfections, giving her to understand that it was not in any way pleasing to Him to see a soul overmuch concerned for its frailties and those lesser faults which human nature cannot always avoid. If these are borne humbly, and with a spirit really conscious of its own misery and entire dependence upon God, the soul is drawn nearer to Our Lord, and He is, as it were, forced to remain with her and help her. ' Cast thy care upon Me (Jesus said to her) and though thine imperfections be numerous, they shall not diminish thy crown as long as thou art humble and obedient.'

One Saturday when Mother Margaret was intending to receive Holy Communion, Our Lady appeared to her at the beginning of Mass, and said :

' This is a day particularly dedicated to me, on which I am much honoured by many little devotions of my servants, on whom also I bestow many favours, as thou shalt experience. Let this day be ever much esteemed by thee, for thou must know that out of a special kindness I have for thee, it is in thy power to obtain much from me upon it.'

At the same moment Mother Margaret saw an angel with the holy Names of Jesus and Mary in glory[1] who stayed beside her all the time of Mass, and at the elevation she saw Our Lord in the Sacred Host. After she had received Holy Communion she had His sufferings during the Passion represented in her heart, and Our Lady explained that she had obtained this favour for her in order that she might know how important it is for servants and spouses of her Divine Son to embrace and love what He so willingly underwent for their sakes.

At the same time she saw numbers of angels adoring Jesus present in her heart, and she was given

[1] This vision was frequently granted to her. See Chapter VII.

to understand that these heavenly spirits adore and reverence their Lord in the hearts of those who receive Him worthily, but that they have such a horror of those who approach Him unworthily that they would destroy them should God's goodness permit it, and that this indignation is felt in proportionate degree even against those who, though receiving Him in a state of grace yet, through distractions or idleness of spirit, neglect to entertain Him in a manner due and suitable to His Divine Presence. This doctrine cast Mother Margaret into a state of fear, which she endeavoured to appease by meditating on the goodness of God, Who bears so patiently with man's ingratitude, and hides His majesty under the sacramental veils in order that all may receive and enjoy Him. Our Lord answered her thought by making known that, although according to the common course of His Divine Providence, His mercies and judgements are kept in an obscurity suitable to our condition in this life; to faithful souls, who frequently receive Him and visit Him in the Blessed Sacrament of the Altar, He often partially unveils His greatness and makes Himself more clearly known, thereby to stir them up to more earnest desires of enjoying His Presence and conversing with Him.

'For thou must know, My child (He said), there is no devotion more grateful to Me than to salute Me frequently in the Blessed Sacrament. Let it therefore be thy constant devotion, both in thy church as often as duty and spare time permit, and with thy heart in those churches where I am least thought of; for by sending extreme desire to be imparting Himself to her and uniting Himself with her, really and so sensibly communicated Himself to her, that she could no ways doubt of it, although she could not express it. Neither was it always in the same manner, for sometimes she saw streams of glory dart from the Blessed Sacrament into her soul. Our Lord said that He often communicated Himself thus to pure souls although they do not perceive it, " for to know it (said He) is a very different favour from possessing it." '

In spite of these consoling experiences Mother Margaret still suffered from distractions and lack of devotion. One morning, being more than usually inattentive before Holy Communion, Our Lady reproved her, saying : ' How comes it thou art so negligent in disposing thyself to receive my Son, whilst He is so solicitous to be doing thee particular favours ? Thou shouldst be always adoring Him, as thou seest these angels do.' Then Margaret's eyes were opened, and she saw her guardian angel amid many others, who satisfied for her deficiencies and moved her to great reverence and devotion. After Communion she saw Our Lord in her heart, Who showed her much favour and said :

' " Know, my child, that thou art no longer in thine own power, for I have taken thy soul from thee and given thee Mine." At these words she saw the Soul of Christ in her, and hers in Him. But she, doubting the truth of this, Our Lord added : " Do not doubt of this, for I can show favours and work wonders where I please in those that will but know I am omnipotent."

Thereupon she saw her heart in the Heart of Jesus, and He said : " See now thy heart is lost in Mine, yet I will shut up Mine in this poor little heart of thine." '

Mother Margaret then saw Our Lord in her heart and all the mysteries of His Sacred Passion engraven upon it, while all His pains were sensibly impressed upon her, so that she felt ' inexpressible torment.' She was supernaturally assured that her heart should retain the impression of Christ's Passion, but not the sensible feeling of His sufferings, for she could not constantly experience this and live.

' Although on these occasions thou findest difficulty in performing thy exterior duties (Our Lord said, referring to a circumstance which often troubled her), thou hast still reason to be thankful to Me, for I do thee a greater favour in not permitting thee to be wholly taken out of thyself by the graces I impart to thee, than by giving them to thee. So long as thou dost gratefully acknowledge it, this favour of super- natural strength necessary to support nature on these occasions shall still be granted thee, unless thine own humiliation or my honour require the contrary.'

Another time when Mother Margaret was kneel- ing in choir with the community during the hour of prayer, she called to mind her many imperfections, especially her desire to be thought well of, a temptation from which she begged Our Lord to deliver her, praying Him to give her a humble heart like those of His servants around her. In reply Our

every person and all she could wish in Him.
Then having flowers in His Hand of great beauty,
He strewed them upon her, saying : " As I now
adorn thee with these flowers, so much more will
this favour, which My Father and I with the Holy
Ghost have bestowed upon thee, become thy
adornment." '

It seemed that Mother Margaret was more than
once favoured with a somewhat similar vision of
the Blessed Trinity, Our Lord expressly greeting
her on one such occasion as : ' Daughter of My
Father, My Spouse and the temple of the Holy
Ghost.' Feeling herself utterly unworthy of His
caresses and unable to bear their sweetness, she cried
out : ' Enlarge my heart, O Lord, or withdraw Thy
favours ! ' Upon this she seemed to see her heart
grown ' vastly great,' with Our Lord in it, and all
in Him, while He asked : ' Art thou satisfied with
this ? ' ' Whatever Thou pleasest, Lord, only let
me be wholly Thine,' she answered, and immediately
saw her heart grow small again, though Our Lord
was in it, and all in Him as before. Then she understood that though her heart was narrow and small
it could yet contain Our Lord, who had shown her
this vision in order that she might see His power.
Then Jesus laying His Hand upon her heart, said :
' I have put my seal upon thy heart. Know I am
wholly thine, and have made thee Mine, and no other
shall ever have place in thee.' After this our blessed
Lady crowned her, greeting her as the spouse of her
Divine Son. ' See, I am thy Mother and Sister
(she said), and I will ever be thy help and strength ;
be sure to endeavour to keep thy soul pure.' At

other times Our Lord enlightened Mother Margaret with regard to His sufferings, showed her His five Sacred Wounds, and warned her that she would have much to suffer in order to become more like Him. ' Stick close to My Cross (He said), this is the only way of truth.' On another occasion He gave the following instruction :

' Suffering is the lesson laid before thee in My life, actions and bitter Passion, and what I have left to sanctify My servants, particularly those who are to belong to Me by a more elevated state of grace and glory. Follow exactly and carefully My inspirations, and comply with them faithfully whatever it costs thee, for perfection does not consist in great desires nor fair words, but in suffering much for Me. Those whom I love, and whom I am resolved to make entirely Mine, I purify by these means, and if they are but faithful in following My steps, I favour them with a particular respect and homage to My life and suffering in their heart.'

On the other hand Mother Margaret was warned by Our Lord not to undertake excessive penances in honour of His Passion, without the express permission of her confessor. One evening she was more than usually fatigued, and found it very tiring to kneel while saying her beads, when Our Lord appeared and after embracing her tenderly, asked her why she did not sit down, as she had been told to do when she was weary. Such acts of obedience (He said) were more pleasing to Him than the respect she tried to pay Him by kneeling. The Holy Prioress at once sat down, and immediately Our Lord seemed to do the same beside her, and while she was all confusion, He explained that little acts, done through obedience, even should they be agreeable to ourselves, are of more value in His sight than many penances of our own invention. Very often those who take satisfaction in their spiritual exercises and penances hinder themselves more in their progress in virtue than those who are remiss in such practices, because they become blinded by self-love. Henceforth Mother Margaret's desires of mortifying herself for love of Jesus should be replaced by abstention from all unusual mortifications and an entire conformity to the commands of her spiritual director.

At this period of her life her own fragile health supplied her with abundant matter for mortification, and about this she was never heard to complain.

One tenth of May, when Mother Margaret during the moments of the Consecration at Mass was making her usual visits to the Five Wounds of Our Lord, the Blessed Virgin appeared to her in a white cloud, showed her Our Lord in glory bearing the marks of His Sacred Wounds, and promised her that whosoever practised the same devotion should be sure of the Last Sacraments and of the use of their senses at death.

Mother Margaret's practice was to visit each Wound offering it for some special intention : the conversion of souls at the *Right Hand ;* at the *Left Hand* the distressed Catholics of England ; at the *Crown of Thorns* the necessities of the Church and the peace of Christian princes ; at the *Sacred Feet* all the humiliations and mortifications God might send that day ; at His *Blessed Side* all friends and particular intentions. When troubled with distractions, and not able to follow this plan, Mother Margaret used to say five *Paters* and *Aves* for the same intentions, and endeavour to accompany Our Lady standing beneath the Cross. The vision thus vouchsafed made her ' both afraid and comforted,' and her note about it continues :

' Our blessed Saviour gave me a sweet countenance and said : " As often as thou dost use this devotion at this time in the Mass, I will give a particular benediction to what thou askest, and if there be not a most pernicious disposition in those for whom thou prayest, they shall find evident comfort when thou prayest for them at that time. Thou seest, and shalt daily find more and more, how pleasing it is to me when thou servest My blessed Mother and dost suffer for Me." '

After she had received Holy Communion at the end of that same Mass, Our Lady again appeared with her Divine Son in her arms, and said : ' Thou wast afraid of my Son in His glory, but now thou canst see Him a little Child in my arms for love of Thee. I am resolved to let thee see what I have prepared for thee in the next life, if thou servest me well.'

With regard to these visions and others still to be related Mother Margaret makes it quite clear that they took place, not through the senses, but in the intellect :

' I cannot say I heard words (she writes), but all this and much more was engraven upon my soul, and though I can say little, yet I find there is more stamped upon my heart and understanding than I have words to express.'

In one of the papers found after her death in Mother Margaret's handwriting was an instruction on humility and simplicity from which the above lines are taken. Our Lord's words as she recorded them fill over three pages in her printed Life, but the substance of them is as follows :

Before God can bestow unusual favours upon a soul it must be prepared by constant fidelity and self-denial, for instance, a feeling of self-satisfaction or pleasure in listening to praise of one's good qualities is a serious obstacle to intimate spiritual favours, because such an attitude of mind robs God of the honour due to Him, from Whom alone all good comes. Idleness is another obstacle, causing in particular great darkness of soul. On the other hand bodily sufferings and infirmities are a help rather than, as many suppose, a hindrance to favours communicated during prayer. 'I have many servants (Our Lord said) that have great desires and even impulses to prayer, which are hindered by the indisposition of their body ; but if they prove faithful I will reward this fidelity with abundant recompense even in this life.' On the other hand, if a soul upon whom God has bestowed special favours is unfaithful, He will exercise His justice most severely upon it. Desires of perfection are not enough, but ' rather puff up to pride ' than please Our Lord, whereas a truly humble soul, who refers everything to God, seeing Him in all ' makes His Omnipotency a prisoner,' so that He is, as it were, forced to make His Will hers, and allow her to dispose of His treasures. With regard to prayer, Mother Margaret was taught that it consists much more in *giving* lovingly to God, than in *receiving* consolations from Him, suffering borne for love of Him being much more meritorious than an abundance of spiritual comfort. Knowledge of its own faults and weaknesses is an indispensable condition in a soul that aspires to perfection, provided it humbly strives to overcome them, knowing that God could, if He so willed, give complete victory, and make these very imperfections become perfections in His sight. Our Lord then made her understand that it is ' a voluntary fault in religious persons if they be not perfect, and proceeds from their want of perseverance in seeking perfection and in overcoming themselves.'

In order to show how pleasing simplicity of heart is to God, and how it opens the soul to free communication with Him, Mother Margaret was one day enlightened about a poor woman who was assisting at Mass in the convent church. Though she was miserable in appearance this woman seemed to Mother Margaret to be encompassed with glory, and Our Lady explained that though her devotions were of the simplest character, they had more power with God than those of some contemplative souls, and that, all unconscious of God's favours as she was, she could, were it necessary, speak with more knowledge of heavenly things than many learned priests.

CHAPTER VII

INTERCOURSE WITH OUR LADY AND THE SAINTS

CANON BEDINGFELD in the preface to his life of Mother Margaret of Jesus says that from her infancy she was ' singularly protected and assisted by the ever blessed Virgin Mary in all her actions, and frequently recreated and comforted with celestial apparitions, which, though noways to be wished for or expected by others, show what Our Lord has reserved for those who sincerely honour His beloved Mother, by whom He will have us seek access to Him.'

He was at pains to prove that the visions granted to this holy Carmelite nun excluded ' all reasonable doubt of illusion or deceit,' and from his own experience shows her to have been of a cheerful and merry disposition, and so even-tempered that she never lost her self-control. He also insists upon the reluctance with which Mother Margaret complied with his command to commit to writing the spiritual favours she received, of which, during her lifetime, the community were entirely ignorant till he himself divulged them after her death :

' As the advice of the Holy Ghost, " *Before death praise no one*," has sealed up my lips for thirty years (he wrote), and hindered me from publishing the simpler perfections and graces of

our venerable Mother Margaret of Jesus, who,
during this time sincerely disclosed to me the
secrets of her happy soul, so now that she has
yielded up her blessed spirit into the hands of
her Divine Spouse, I think my obligation equally
great to comply with the impulse of the same
Holy Spirit who requires that we should praise
men after their consummation.'

What is here recorded is, therefore, given on the
authority of Canon Bedingfeld, who expressly
declared at the beginning of his *Life of Margaret
Mostyn* that the incidents were derived only from
human authority, and that he submitted everything
to the judgement of Holy Mother Church.

One day when Mother Margaret was much
troubled with distractions Our Lady sent an angel
of extraordinary beauty to comfort her. This angel
was her own little sister who assured her that
she was in heaven with their father, who was
greatly rejoiced by seeing his little girl in as much
glory as many others who had served God for a
much longer time. Mr. Mostyn had privately
determined to dedicate this little daughter to Our
Lady as a Carmelite, if she were willing, but ' as
this would not have happened if I had lived (she
explained), Our Blessed Lady called me to herself
before I was capable of displeasing her.' Then,
smiling on Mother Margaret, she added : ' How
happy you are to be able to merit so much ! '
' But, dear Sister, shall I do so ? ' her elder sister
replied, upon which she again said : ' You are
happy,' and asked Margaret to praise Our Lady
for her because, though she had done nothing

while on earth to merit great glory, yet, because she was devout to Our Lady ' above the knowledge of her years,' the blessed Virgin had obtained for her the privilege of an increase in accidental joy and glory, whenever she herself was praised.

Among other favours Mother Margaret some-times heard heavenly music. It brought her so much consolation that one day she asked Our Lady to obtain that she might hear it eternally. The blessed Virgin immediately appeared to her saying :

'Fear not, as long as thou dost obey, and knowest that thou art poor and deservest nothing, thy desires shall be granted, in pledge of which I here bring thee My Son. Keep him company and desire him to prepare thy heart for Com-munion to-morrow, when thou shalt hear Mass with as much jubilee as can be imagined and more than thou couldst ever have conceived heaven itself to be.'

At this Mother Margaret was puzzled, thinking that no music could exceed in beauty what she had already heard, but Our Lady, laying her hand upon her head, answered : ' My child, how little dost thou know what is to be enjoyed there ! ' At that moment the convent bell rang for Vespers. Mother Margaret rose at once, hesitated for a second what to do as the Blessed Virgin did not move, then went straight to the choir. There Our Lady met her with the Infant Jesus in her arms. ' Because thou didst leave me to obey the bell (she said), I bring thee my Son : hadst thou done otherwise, thou wouldst have lost this pleasure. Take Him, He shall remain with thee till I fetch Him.' With that the Mother of God vanished, but Mother Margaret saw the Divine Infant in her own heart, and yet at the same time embracing her. She adored Him, and was filled with sorrow for what, she felt, was the wickedness of her life. But the Infant Jesus only smiled, saying that nothing of all that should hinder His obliging His blessed Mother by comforting her, and that she must think herself a little child for so He delighted to have her. This she understood to mean that she must practise great simplicity with an entire unconcern of what others thought of her, being occupied solely with His love.

The Sacred Infant stayed with her till three o'clock, at which hour she was due with the novices. As she knelt with them saying the Litany of Loreto, Our Lady appeared accompanied by an angel, and asked her if she was willing to part with her Son. Amazement and confusion prevented Mother Margaret from answering, and the Infant Jesus turning to His Mother said : ' She is unwilling to let Us go.' Our Lady questioned her a second time, but she could still say nothing, only wishing to be taken out of this uncertain and dangerous life. To this thought her heavenly Mother replied : ' Thou dost not know what thou desirest, for didst thou but understand the value and merit of one act of obedience, neither human respect nor anything whatever thou mightest suffer in this life would hinder thee from practising the most difficult ones, or prevail upon thee to omit the very least.' Then turning towards the angel Our Lady asked : ' Dost thou know this Angel ? ' and when Mother Margaret recollected having seen him before, she added : ' He shall be with thee in all thy necessities, and thou shalt often see him with the Names of Jesus and Mary in glory,' whereupon the Divine Infant lifted His hand and blessed her, and with His holy Mother vanished from her sight.

On another occasion when Our Lady appeared to her during Mass, Mother Margaret saw the whole Order of Carmel occupied in singing her praises and those of her Divine Son. It happened that one of the novices was absent, and while she went to fetch her, the angel of the Holy Names took her place in the choir. On her return, he bowed and moved aside, and immediately the whole choir seemed filled with heavenly music, and Our Lady said: 'She is of our number.' At this Mother Margaret wished to know if it was the same with the rest of the community, and instantly she saw all the Sisters present in the Heart of the Divine Infant, who said: 'I repose in their hearts, and therefore their place of rest is in Mine, as thou dost see.'

Being once at work with the Sisters during the hour of recreation, she happened to rise first when the bell rang the *Angelus*. Whilst she was saying it, she saw Our Lady with her Divine Child, Who gave His blessing to all. Our Lady then said: 'Because thou didst stand up first at the sound of the bell, I will give thee my Son during the whole time of recreation.' This gave her so much joy that she was inclined to leave off what she was doing in order to attend to her Divine Guest, but Jesus let her understand that she pleased Him best when she was busy with the duty of the moment, which was no hindrance to His union with her.

Even while she was asleep when obedience

prescribed it (He explained), she was performing an action as pleasing to Him as any other, for He kept watch in her heart where He would continue to impart His graces according to the measure of her obedience.

It was Our Lady who protected Mother Margaret when she was attacked by the devil. One day as she was going to pray before a favourite statue of the Mother of God, she was stopped by a dense black cloud. Supposing it to be caused by the devil, she tried to bless herself but found she could not move her arm. This frightened her so much that she turned back, but saw an angel (as she supposed) who told her that the devil was in the cloud and would carry her to Hell if she wrote or spoke any more of her favours and visions.

For some time previous to this, the holy Prioress had been tempted to disbelieve the favours showered upon her, but had been reassured about them by Our Lady. This put her on her guard, and rather than encounter this lying spirit, she determined to pass through the cloud and made a cross in the air with her head. Immediately her arm was free, and signing herself with the Cross, she found the cloud dispersed and was able to enter the room where the statue was venerated. Her doubts about her spiritual state still oppressed her, and she made up her mind to burn all her papers and undeceive her confessor, at the same time accepting any penance he might impose upon her. At this point in her reflections, Our Lady came to her promising always to defend her, and, showing her the false angel as an ugly black dog, said : ' This is he who would hinder thee from crediting my favours.' The sight of this frightful object made Mother Margaret still more afraid, and she crept towards the place where Our Lady stood. The black dog did not attempt to follow her, whereupon she was thrown into fresh doubts, wondering whether she saw Our Lady or not. Then the Blessed Virgin cast her mantle over her right side, saying : ' It is I, my child. I am the Mother of God. Know that this devil is forced to stay here to his own confusion, and from this time, in token of my presence, I command him never to come upon thy right side, so that, let him be in never so much glory, so long as thou dost obey and art faithful to me, thou shalt never be so far deceived as not to be able to help thyself and discern his illusions.'

One day when a votive Mass of the Assumption was being offered in thanksgiving for some favour, Our Lady showed Mother Margaret, in answer to her wish, the whole Order of Mount Carmel in Heaven standing beside her, all so glorious that she thought it impossible to imagine anything more resplendent. Yet, upon studying the faces of the nuns, she could not recognize any she had known. Then Our Lady showed her Mother Anne of the Ascension (Worsley) and all her other Sisters, assuring her that she had them wholly under her care and that they were as dear to her as the rest. Afterwards she was given to understand that it was, in some sort, a sign of predestination to belong to the Carmel of Lierre, or indeed to the Order of Discalced Carmelites, and that its members were, by a special privilege, rarely tempted against holy purity, and hence enjoyed places in heaven near Our Blessed Lady. Mother Teresa of Jesus Mary,

sister to Mother Anne of the Ascension, was pointed
out among others by Our Lady as having great
glory because in life she struggled bravely against
persistent temptations. Our Lady then took a
girdle from her own waist and put it round Mother
Margaret as a pledge of her special protection.

Mother Anne Worsley had been professed on
Whit-Sunday and she instilled into all her Sisters
a great devotion to the Holy Ghost. Mother
Margaret, though one of the last whom she received,
always cherished the teaching of her first Prioress,
and prepared very carefully every year for the Feast
of Pentecost. One year, on the vigil of this feast,
she was awakened as usual by her angel guardian
and immediately saw Our Lady, who gave her a
blessing. During her hour of prayer she begged
her heavenly Mother's help in preparing her soul
to receive the Holy Ghost, and Our Lady appeared
more distinctly, and

> ' thrusting the little Infant into her arms, said :
> " Here is my Son, observe Him, and He will
> teach thee how to prepare thyself. St. Joseph
> gained all his sanctity by contemplating this
> Blessed Child, and now thou hast Him in thine
> arms and heart, thou hast the same in thy power.
> Do not let Him go, therefore, till thou knowest
> how to prepare thyself for the coming of the
> Holy Ghost." '

The Divine Infant remained with her, telling her
only to have faith and humility and she should
receive His Divine Spirit. After Holy Communion
she was allowed to see how the Holy Ghost was

imparted to all the nuns in the choir, each receiving a greater or lesser share of His gifts according to her dispositions. On the morning of Pentecost she again saw Our Lady accompanied by St. Teresa and Mother Anne of the Ascension, and was told that all present should know that she had received the Holy Ghost in a special way. According to custom, when the sequence *Veni Sancte Spiritus* was intoned during Mass, a wild dove was let loose in the choir, bearing bits of parchment cut into the form of tongues of fire on which were written the gifts of the Holy Ghost and which were thus scattered on the floor. The dove flew first to a statue of Our Lady and then perched on Mother Margaret's head till the Elevation, when it fluttered to the lectionary and remained there. Just at the moment when the Sacred Host was elevated, the choir became filled with glory in which Mother Margaret saw ' a dove betwixt silver and gold from which there came streams of glory.' This seemed to descend upon her head, and, according to her inward desire, she felt its weight, while by fluttering its wings it made a sort of wind which filled her with delight. All this time Our Lady held her by the hand, and St. Teresa and Mother Anne of the Ascension stood close by, and, thus encompassed with glory, she went up to receive Holy Communion. After she had communicated she saw the same dove in her soul, as well as Our Blessed Lord, Who (as she thought) carried her to His Eternal Father, Who breathed into her the Holy Ghost. Our Lord assured her that the Holy Ghost would always remain with her and give her a right understanding, and it was this gift that was written on the piece of parchment which she afterwards picked up.

When the Office of Sext began the wild dove came back to her, this time alighting near her heart for a second or two, then resting again upon her head :

'It seemed to cover her once or twice with its wings (says the MS. Life), as if taking leave, and soon after fled away and became so wild, that it was near a quarter of an hour before they could catch it to send it home.

All that day she was favoured with the presence of Our Lady and St. Teresa, so that in company it was as much as she could do to contain herself, and dissemble her interior joy, for every place seemed full of God, and wherever she was, either in choir or recreation, she heard angelical music notwithstanding her endeavours to divert and amuse herself, lest the Sisters should perceive anything.'

Mother Margaret once described the heavenly music she so often heard, and said it was not like that of any instrument she knew, though she was naturally fond of music and sometimes accused herself of self-indulgence by taking pleasure in listening to it. This celestial harmony (she said) was sometimes like 'sweet curious voices very still and sweet yet shrill and loud,' and that she could hear the singing distinctly even when others were speaking or someone was making a noise. This favour was granted, Our Lady once explained, to wean her from all love of earthly things, and as a reward for the mortification she practised in regard to earthly music. During her first months as Novice-Mistress Mother Margaret suffered much from depression, and even had thoughts against her vocation. This continued up to the feast of Our Lady's Immaculate Conception. On December 7th, as she was passing the refectory after assisting at the First Vespers of the Feast and begging Our Lady's help, she heard in a clear sweet voice the word *Adsum*, ' I am here.' This changed all her sadness into joy and peace. This was one of her earliest favours, and in writing of it, she notes that she did not understand who it was who spoke until Canon Bedingfeld explained that it was Our Lady.

It was Canon Bedingfeld also who left on record the devotion of the *Ten Aves* taught to Mother Margaret by the Blessed Virgin. A similar devotion had been revealed by Our Lady just a century earlier to Blessed Joan, Duchess of Berri,[1] the foundress of the Annunciade Nuns, and the recital of the *Aves* had been enriched by one of the Popes with many indulgences. However, Canon Bedingfeld left, in his own handwriting, an assurance that Mother Margaret had never heard of either the revelation or the devotion.

One Quinquagesima Sunday after receiving from Our Lord some special instructions about honouring His Sacred Passion during Lent, Mother Margaret was troubled because, as she explained, when the Gospel was finished, she found her beads also finished, and she was not sure whether she had said them or not, as her thoughts were not on them.

---

[1] Blessed Joan of France was the daughter of Louis XI. Her nuns have a convent at St. Margaret-at-Cliffe, Kent.

At that moment, Our Lady appeared, and embracing her, showed her as the fruit of her recitation of the beads the mysteries of the Passion imprinted in her heart, just as she had seen them before. After reassuring her that her devotions had been well made, Our Lady added: 'I will teach thee a devotion most pleasing to me, which thou shalt make daily this Lent in honour of my virtues.'

The devotion thus taught by Our Lady consisted of Ten *Aves* in honour of each virtue to be meditated upon, followed by a *Laudate* in thanksgiving for all the privileges granted to her through its practice. Mother Margaret's paper relating Our Lady's instructions is very full, giving the contemplation suitable to each virtue thus honoured, and the lesson to be derived from the way the Blessed Virgin practised it. A summary of her paper will suffice here.

Devotion of the Ten Aves

1. *Our Lady's Purity*. 'How can this be done, since I know not man.'
   The dignity and perfection of holy purity.

2. *Our Lady's Prudence*. 'She considered how great this Salutation might be.'
   Necessity of this spiritual prudence for those who aspire to perfection.

3. *Our Lady's Humility*. 'Behold the handmaid of the Lord.'
   The value in God's sight of lowliness of spirit and willingness to serve others.

4. *Our Lady's Fidelity.* ' Blessed art thou, because thou hast believed.'
   The advantages of a lively faith, which should be earnestly begged of God.

5. *Our Lady's Gratitude.* ' My soul doth magnify the Lord.'
   How readily Our Lady helps those who honour her, and refer all to God.

6. *Our Lady's Obedience.* ' Be it done unto me according to Thy Word.'
   The dignity and value of religious obedience.

7. *Our Lady's Poverty.* ' She laid Him in a manger.'
   The use Our Lady made of poverty at the birth of her Divine Son, and how religious should imitate her in this virtue.

8. *Our Lady's Patience.* ' Thy father and I have sought thee sorrowing.'
   Patience in times of aridity and trouble.

9. *Our Lady's Charity.* ' They have no wine.'
   Consideration for others.

10. *Our Lady's Constancy.* ' There stood by the Cross of Jesus His Mother.'
    Constancy in suffering, which gives souls a share in Our Lady's power over the merits of Her Divine Son.

When Mother Margaret had finished the last *Laudate* of the above devotion, Our Lady embraced her and promised great graces and favours to those who honour her in this way, especially by making them share in those ten virtues, which she would imprint in their hearts. At the end of her account the holy Prioress wrote that Our Lady wished Canon Bedingfeld himself to make use of this way of honouring her, especially when he visited the shrine of Our Lady of Slues or Cluyes, a miraculous statue held in great veneration in Lierre.[1] This image of Our Lady of Cluyes used, on certain great feasts, to be brought in procession to the English Carmel. On one such occasion it happened that Mother Ursula of All Saints was lying in the infirmary dangerously ill. The statue was carried to her bedside, and she was instantly cured.

Other visions granted to Mother Margaret made her familiar with God's Saints. She saw St. Joseph more than once, St. Augustine, St. Mary of Egypt, St. Peter of Alcantara, St. Francis of Assisi, St. Francis of Sales and many others. St. Francis of Assisi appeared to her with his whole Order. She distinguished clearly the stigmata in his hands and feet, which did not appear as she had seen them in pictures, but as rays of glory quite different from those that surrounded him. She understood that the devotion Mother Margaret of St. Teresa had to him had won his special protection for the Lierre Carmel, and that anyone truly devoted to him will obtain the virtues of humility and simplicity which he practised in a high degree. Canon Bedingfeld gives an account of some other points made known to Mother Margaret Mostyn by this great saint :

' St. Francis said that though he had many most eminent Saints in his Order when he was on

[1] Our Lady of the Cloister (Dutch, *clues*) venerated in a Dominican Convent in Lierre.

earth, yet there were still living many as great, and in some kind greater, which she understood to be a privilege granted to all Founders of Orders, who merit even in this life that Almighty God, of His goodness, raises up from time to time other saints to uphold their spirit, and to do that which oftentimes would not have been fit in the beginning of the Order, and which afterwards contributes to its preservation and greater good.

The splendour of this saint, and the glory he received from all the different branches of his Institution, for all that profess his rule seemed equally near to him, was so great that she seemed in a manner out of herself in beholding it, and in amaze began to think that there was no glory in Heaven comparable to what this Order enjoyed. But being favoured also by Our Lord with a sight of other religious Orders she was equally astonished, for every one did seem to possess, though in a different kind, so much glory that she thought those she actually looked upon so far surpassed all others that nothing else could be greater, or in any way comparable to it. " This," said Our Blessed Lord, " is Heaven and this the glory I impart to My servants " : and added that if there were as many millions more, He could as easily glorify Himself in giving them different degrees of glory. She observed that the crowns of all these Orders were not only different, but some far superior to others in glory : and that those Orders whose principal Institute is recollection and union with God by prayer were in a particular degree glorified in seeing and knowing more of Almighty God than others, which made her think the happiness of a Teresian to surpass all others. This Our Lord gave her to understand was the happy situation of the Blessed in heaven, who possessing all they desire, conceive the highest opinion of their own glory without envy or ambition to higher, which He let her experience. For when she beheld the Order of Carmel she thought there was no glory like unto what it enjoyed, though when she looked upon others it seemed to her that nothing could be greater than theirs, yet she had no ambition nor desire of any other, but that of a Teresian.

She observed, however, that though the crowns which distinguished each Religious Order were common and uniform to all those who were of that Order, yet as they were rewarded each one according to their private merits, they were quite different from one another in point of glory, some exceeding others beyond all comparison, according to the various virtues they had excelled in, and the perfection they had attained to during their life.'

Our Lord sometimes enlightened Mother Margaret with regard to the spiritual state of persons still living, especially that of certain priests. Thus she was allowed to see the crown prepared for Canon Bedingfeld, and one day during Mass she was shown how certain faults committed by the celebrant hindered him from receiving the full benefit of the Holy Sacrifice he was offering to God. This made the holy Carmelite anxious about the state of several priests she had known before her entrance into religion, and who were reported to be leading imperfect lives. She hastened to recommend to God these souls and those of others in a like state, and Our Lord showed her that those she held in less esteem were, in reality, more pleasing to Him than others whom she thought very holy, and made her understand that a good intention combined with patience under the unfavourable judgements of others often atones for many small faults, provided all disedification is avoided. She was also allowed to see the dangerous spiritual state of the priest who had given her her First Holy Communion, of whom she had a very high opinion, so that she began to pray fervently for him.

Another day she saw in great glory Father Andrew White, S.J., *alias* Clayton, who had been her confessor in Hopland. With him were both Our Lord and His Blessed Mother, who assured her that he was a very great servant of theirs, and that he had done more for the English Carmel in Antwerp by his humble prayers, than a less prayerful man of greater natural abilities would have achieved. Mother Margaret had not esteemed Father Andrew very highly, thinking he did not understand her, and that he thought too well of her, but Our Lady now assured her that what he had said to her was true, and if at any time he had not understood her, it was so allowed by Our Lord in order to prevent him from trying to keep her from leaving Antwerp.

On more than one occasion Mother Margaret was allowed to see the devil tempting members of her community. Among the latter was Mary Basson, a Dutch lady, who entered in 1650, taking the name

Agnes Mary of St. Joseph. This nun Mother Margaret frequently saw surrounded by devils, so that she prayed very specially for her to Our Blessed Lady. One day while she was thus engaged, Our Lady appeared to her and promised to help the afflicted Sister, provided she endeavoured to help herself. The devils meanwhile continued tempting Sister Agnes, but without injuring her either in soul or body, and Our Lady showed Mother Margaret how impotent they were, saying : 'Trust therefore in me, and be assured that this good Sister is under my special protection, and so dear to me that nothing shall do her harm.'

Notwithstanding this, the Prioress did not feel drawn to Sister Agnes though she continued to pray for her. Our Lord rewarded this act of charity by appearing to Mother Margaret one day after she had received Holy Communion, and saying :

'This is a pure act of obedience and charity and thou shalt see how pleasing it is to Me, for although thou hast no affection for this Sister, she is most dear to Me, and I will make her so to thee, and I will teach thee how to rejoice even in the sufferings of thy friends and Mine as much as in their prosperity, because both are equally pleasing to My Father, and depend upon His Divine Will ; for He is as much glorified and honoured in exercising His servants by tribulations and crosses, as in bestowing upon them rewards and favours.'

Sister Agnes of St. Joseph overcame all her temptations, and lived in the faithful observance of her Rule until January 18th, 1692, when she passed to her eternal reward.

Some time before Mother Margaret Mostyn became Prioress, Mother Margaret of St. Teresa desired her to pray that she might know whether her mother was in heaven. In answer to this request, Our Lord told the younger Margaret that Mrs. Downes had been admitted into heaven through a Mass which was said for her at Antwerp, and that her father was also freed from Purgatory through the Masses and prayers procured by their friends, as well as all her sisters except one named Anne, who still needed twenty-five Masses to set her free. Margaret told this to her Superior, and the next night she was cruelly beaten by the devil, who appeared in a hideous shape. After some time Our Lady came and comforted her, and showed her Anne's soul all in flames, yet submissive and at peace in her sufferings, though this did not mitigate her pain. This sight upset the young religious so much that she could not settle to anything, until during the conventual Mass she saw this soul standing close to the priest as he read the Gospel, while Our Lady and St. Teresa also seemed to be there. At first Anne seemed to be still suffering, but at the elevation of the Sacred Host, Sister Margaret saw her in white raiment, making a bow to her to let her Reverend Mother know that she was now in Heaven. Anne Downes had married a Protestant named William Warren, and only lived a few months after the birth of her little daughter, Mary Teresa, whom she had dedicated to Our Lady. After her mother's death the child was brought up by one of her aunts, a

maiden lady named Martha. When Mary Teresa
was six years old Martha Downes died, and in
order to keep the little girl from her Protestant
relations, she was sent to Mother Margaret of St.
Teresa, who placed her with a good Catholic lady
in Lierre to be educated. It was two years after
this that Mother Margaret Mostyn had seen Anne
Warren in glory, and the account given by her to
her Reverend Mother was unexpectedly confirmed
by the latter's little niece. The last of the twenty-
five Masses said for her mother's release from
Purgatory was offered at the shrine of Our Lady of
Clues. Mary Teresa was present, but did not know
for whom the Holy Sacrifice was being offered.
Towards the end of Mass she called out to the
Béguine who took care of her : ' I see my mother
all in white go up to Heaven, and she says I shall
come to her and something about my being a nun
which I cannot remember.' Later on, when relating
this to her aunt, Mary Teresa described her mother
so minutely and clearly that Mother Margaret of
St. Teresa recognized it as a description of her sister.
Though the child had no remembrance of her
mother, her account never varied and she grew
so excited in telling the nuns all about it, that she
was taken home in a high fever. However she
soon got over this, and when she was fourteen she
begged to be received as a novice. Mother Margaret
Mostyn was then Prioress, and told her she was not
old enough, but Mary Teresa accidentally met the
Bishop in the Carmel, where he had come to preside
over the elections, and so well did she plead her
own cause, that his Lordship allowed her to be
clothed with Our Lady's habit as soon as she

turned fifteen. He told Mother Margaret to have particular care of her, and as soon as she attained the canonical age of seventeen, she made her profession as Mary Teresa of Jesus, March 19th, 1660. The Lierre Necrology says :

' Sister Mary Teresa died on October 4th, 1696, aged 54, a person very serviceable to the community, endowed with good parts, leaving her Sisters a rare example of solid virtue.'

Further knowledge was granted to Margaret Mostyn about her Reverend Mother's deceased relatives. One of these was a wild young man who was to be detained in Purgatory until certain specified suffrages were offered for his release. Our Lady also said that she had obtained the early death of this young man for the sake of his father and mother, for had he lived he would not have saved his soul. Another time she understood that Sister Eugenia's brother was in Heaven, but his wife would remain in Purgatory until three pilgrimages had been made for her to Our Lady of Duffel, because she had promised to make three pilgrimages to St. Winifred's Well, and had failed to fulfil her promise.

Mother Margaret was also once told by Our Lady to send word to the Subprioress in Hopland, then Mother Margaret of the Angels (Walton), that her mother was in Purgatory and asked that the following devotions should be offered in order to obtain her release : Nine Masses to be said for the souls in Purgatory, because these had been promised during the sickness of one of her sons, and had not as yet been said; a pilgrimage to Our Lady of Sichem, where an offering of ten shillings was to be made; and lastly a votive Mass of thanksgiving to be offered in the Antwerp Carmel, at which the Sub-prioress was to thank God for the favour of learning her mother's needs. All this was duly performed, and Mother Margaret Mostyn saw Mrs. Walton's soul admitted into Heaven with fourteen others on he following Trinity Sunday.

One day Mother Margaret was privileged to see her own place in Heaven not far from St. Teresa, but nearer to Our Lady. She also saw the place prepared for her own mother, which was higher than the one obtained by her grandmother on account of the hindrance the latter had placed to her becoming a Carmelite, and some vanity in her manner of educating her. Mother Margaret felt troubled at this, but immediately she seemed to hear a shrill voice saying : ' I am well, and have all I desire.' Afterwards Our Lady explained that Margaret's grandmother received new glory by every virtuous action she performed which sprang from the principles old Mrs. Fox had instilled into her young mind.

' I let thee know these things (Our Lady said), in order that the world may see how much it imports to teach children vocal prayers, and devotion to me, and also that parents may take warning how to bring up their children, not hindering them from entering religion.'

An instruction regarding England must conclude this account of Mother Margaret's graces.

St. Teresa had appeared to her and after blessing

her, desired her to pray for England and her Order there :

'Pray much for England (said the saint), and pray with confidence for you may obtain much. When I was in the world I ever had a great desire and ambition to help that poor country, and now, if I could be impatient for anything in heaven it would be to obtain great blessings for England ; I will help in a particular way any of that country who in their afflictions make use of devotions to me.'

Saint Teresa also promised that England should profit spiritually by the good done in the Carmel in Lierre, and told Mother Margaret to keep herself very lowly in order that God might do great good through her, and that her name would be venerated not only in her own community, but by many others.

May this little sketch of her holy life help to bring about the fulfilment of Our Lady's promise.

EPILOGUE

THE firm and gentle rule of Mother Margaret of Jesus was continued by her sister, who was unanimously elected to succeed her. Of Mother Ursula of All Saints a Darlington MS. has the following note:

> ' Many and great were the favours that marked her life, but as she survived her confessor, Father Bedingfeld, few comparatively are known. She was a saintly Superior in all, a worthy model of her sister in inexhaustible charity, striking humility, and every virtue, we may truly say.'

The community at Lierre became a nursery of Saints as the lives of the Sisters attest. From the foundation of the house these have been carefully preserved, and make most interesting and edifying reading. The family name of each Sister is given, with those of her parents, the dates of her clothing and profession, together with any facts of special interest concerning her life before she entered, her work and virtues as a professed Carmelite, and the date and circumstances of her death.

In 1755 it is recorded that Anne Housman (daughter of James and Anne Housman, *née* Searle)

> ' took the holy habit of Our Blessed Lady of Mount Carmel in our Convent of Lier in Brabant on August 19th, and made her holy profession on the 20th August, 1756.'

She was called in religion Mary Anne Bernard of St. Teresa. Born in London in 1739, Anne Housman went to Lierre at the age of ten, and was sent to Mechlin to be educated. She learnt Flemish as well as French and had a particular gift for conducting business. A few days before her profession the Carmel in Lierre received two precious relics of Our Lady and St. Joseph which were carried in solemn procession through the town and then brought to the Convent by the Dean and Chapter of the Collegiate Church of St. Gomare, ' the *Te Deum* being solemnly performed in music.'

In 1772 Mother Mary Bernard was elected Prioress, an office she held by continuous re-elections until 1810.

Thus it fell to her to make the momentous decision of transferring her community to England in 1794. The first decade of her priorate passed peacefully enough, and Mother Mary Bernard's business capacity enabled her to put the financial affairs of the Convent into good order, which had before been ' in a very embarrassed state.'

The first interruption of this tranquillity occurred in 1782, when the Emperor Joseph II arranged for the suppression of many convents throughout his dominions. It was not known at first that those of English communities would be exempt from this decree, and Mother Mary Bernard made arrangements for her nuns to go to St. Denis, near Paris, where Mother Teresa of St. Augustine (Madame Louise of France) was Prioress. This proved to be unnecessary :

'Yet fearing new storms might arise (says the MS.), our worthy Superior took every precaution prudence suggested to secure the temporals, and sold the church plate, reserving only what was necessary. During about 12 years from anno 1782 until 1794 the community were in continual alarm.'

The frequent publication of edicts despoiling churches and religious houses of their property, and abrogating their ancient rights and privileges occasioned a breach between the Imperial Court of Austria and the Netherlands. Many of the wealthier families in Lierre, fearing disaster, brought their valuables to Mother Mary Bernard, begging her to keep them till peace was restored. This caused her great anxiety, for in some cases she felt it impossible to refuse, and ' glad she was when the owners got them back again,' as soon as Francis II restored peace and order.

The respite from bloodshed lasted, however, only a short time. By 1792 the French armies were again overrunning the Netherlands, bringing fear and devastation in their train.

' One of the regiments was marching before our Convent (says a MS. chronicle) and was going to force the gate, when Father Roby [chaplain to the Carmelite nuns, then quite a young priest], who was a person of extraordinary courage, stood before it, resolved to defend his dear children at the expense of his own life. The soldiers, struck at his courage, desisted and left us quiet, but to prevent any further molestation Father Roby went to one of the French generals (an American) [sic], who graciously received him, and promised his protection. This General sent

MOTHER MARY ANNE BERNARD HOUSMAN
(From a miniature preserved at Carmel House, Darlington.)

Facing page 134

a guard of soldiers to protect our Convent, and he himself came once or twice into the Convent, kindly assuring us that as long as he stayed in Lierre he would not allow any insult to be offered to us.'

The same MS. relates that the French retired from the Netherlands quite suddenly, and that General Dumouriez compelled the soldiers to restore the plate taken from the various churches. But peace was not of long duration, for the French armies soon returned and took possession of the country in 1794.

' The religious of the different monasteries fled as best they could (the chronicle continues). The Augustinian nuns of Bruges took refuge in Lierre, only to accompany our Sisters a fortnight later in their hurried flight. On 2nd July by way of Breda the community reached Rotterdam, where several other English nuns of different Orders had found a temporary refuge before embarking for England. On 4th July, our Sisters with some Flemish Carmelites, who had sought refuge and found a permanent Home with us on the destruction of their Convent, together with Father Roby and a Flemish priest, took shipping for London. There a friend [Mrs. Cater] received part of the Community, and the rest were invited by Mr. Charles Butler [nephew of the great Alban Butler] to Red Lion Square where he had a domestic chapel. There they could have daily Mass, keep choir, and perform all conventual duties, and for 9 weeks were provided with all the necessaries of life *gratis*. The rest of the

Sisters had to assist at Mass in the public chapels of the City.

When we landed on July 6th in the evening Mother Mary Bernard, with two of the community, going from the ship to get a coach were surprised by a mob. One, more bold than the rest, rudely took hold of the arms of the Sisters, insolently pulling them along, but they took no hurt being, as we believe, singularly protected by Our Blessed Lady.'

In vain did the Mother Prioress seek in the environs of London for a house which could be converted into a Carmel. Nothing suitable could be found. About the end of August, Sir John Lawson offered the nuns a home at Brough Hall, Yorkshire, while he himself went house-hunting for them in the neighbourhood. Part of the community started north on September 4th, and received 'a most welcome and cordial reception from Sir John and his lady.' On September 8th Mother Mary Bernard went to see a house in St. Helen's Auckland. Though small, it was suitable for a convent, and the nuns took possession on September 14th. The first Mass was said in this 'new Carmel of Lierre' on September 18th, and on the feast of Our Lady of Mercy the whole community reassembled there, much to their consolation and delight. One of Sir John Lawson's grandchildren, Grace Lawson, entered at Carmel House, Darlington, on October 15th, 1862, and was professed as Mary Bridget Aloysia of Jesus Crucified the following year. The Darlington necrology contains a long notice about her and her saintly family, to various members of which the nuns owed so much.

'This dear Sister (says the MS.) was born at Richmond in Yorkshire on the 17th June, 1831. She was the daughter of Wm. Wright, Esqre and of his wife Clarinda Lawson, the only child and daughter of John Lawson Esqre of York (Physician). Through her as heiress in the female line as well as in his own right on his mother's side, her Father, soon after our dear Sister's birth, came in for the property and Estate of Brough Hall, near Catterick, where he removed with his young family, assuming also the name Lawson.'

After noting that the baronetcy was revived in favour of Grace's father, the MS. describes life at Brough Hall which 'resembled rather a religious House than a worldly dwelling,' so that the future Carmelite grew up in a thoroughly Catholic atmosphere. Of her four brothers, the second, William, entered the Society of Jesus 'where by his virtue and learning, as well as by the many services he rendered to the Society, he soon distinguished himself as one of its most valuable members.' Grace was such a sturdy child that she used to relate with glee how 'the butler, on being taken to see her, exclaimed: "She's the bonniest bearn among um. Not at all like a gentleman's child!"' However this early promise was not fulfilled for the little girl suffered from weakness in the lower limbs and was never at any time really strong. Her father's benefactions to the Carmelites and the beautiful chapel of St. Paulinus which he built on his estate so reduced his income that the family lived in Italy for some years. One winter was spent at Albano, near Rome.

> ' It was here little Grace often went to pray before a statue of St. Albert in the church of the Carmelite Friars, begging him, in her innocent simplicity, to allow her one day to follow the Rule he had given them.'

On returning to England she was sent to the Bar Convent, York, for a short time, but soon went home to nurse her mother who had become deaf, and very blind. Yet the old lady kept the management of the house in her own hands, and Grace had to submit everything to her. Her mother could read only white characters on a dark background, so each item of housekeeping had to be carefully written on a large slate, all letters received being copied word for word in the same way. When in 1862 God called her mother to Himself, Sir William Lawson was ailing, but Bishop Cornthwaite decided that Grace should wait no longer, but confide her father to the care of her eldest brother, John, and his wife, who were already living at Brough Hall. To the end of his life Sir William continued to bestow gifts on Carmel House, almost the last (for he died soon after) was a beautiful statue of the Immaculate Conception in the nun's garden in memory of Grace's profession, she herself having previously given one of St. Joseph, as well as having paid for improvements in the Carmel itself.

Grace chose the name Mary Bridget because it had been that of a holy lay-sister, a former dairymaid at Brough Hall, who was the first novice received after the nuns came to England. A year before her death Sister Mary Bridget Lawson was warned by a holy Franciscan friar that her course was nearly run. She lived about a year longer, and gave up her pure soul to God on St. Stephen's Day, December 26th, 1885, aged 54. The nuns noted a happy coincidence in her dying on that day, for apparently it was on August 3rd, the feast of the Finding of St. Stephen, that she left home in 1862. The Darlington MSS. include a letter written on that occasion to the future Sister Mary Bridget by Bishop Grant ' of blessed memory ' :

' To-morrow will be the feast of St. Stephen, and you must ask him to obtain for you the ardent and generous love which made the Heavens open to his eyes, with Jesus at the Right Hand of the Father. It is the same Jesus for whom you are leaving home, and in leaving your earthly home you will see the Eternal Father Who wishes to espouse you to His own dear Son, and to give you power to help and support and strengthen your father in all his sacrifices. I feel as if I saw Sister Bridget [the lay-sister] coming from the side of St. Teresa's throne to help you to follow her from Brough to become a daughter of Mount Carmel.'

The life of Sister Mary Bridget (Lawson) has been given at some length because the present nuns of Carmel House, Darlington, wish (like their predecessors) to put on record ' the immense obligation their community owes to this noble and inestimable Family.'

Just ten years after their arrival at St. Helen's Auckland, the nuns, still under the leadership of Mother Mary Bernard, removed in 1804 to Cocken Hall, an estate belonging to Mr. Ibittson. Mother Mary Bernard died in Cocken Hall 'on March 26th, 1827 aged 88, a jubilarian 21 years.' She was succeeded as Prioress on April 30th, 1810, by Mother Clare of Jesus Crucified (Dalton). Jane Dalton's family belonged to Lancashire and she was received at Lierre on November 21st, 1774, a few months before she was seventeen, but owing to the restriction made by the Empress Maria Teresa of Austria, she was not able to make her profession till she was twenty-five. Her birthday was December 28th, 1757, so she made her vows on January 1st, 1783, having given great edification during her long noviceship. She was succeeded in office by Mother Mary Aloysia Francis of the Sacred Heart, Esther Housman, who (also at the age of seventeen) entered at Lierre in 1782, but was professed on March 18th, 1789, the Emperor Joseph having abridged the time of probation by one year. Even then her reception of the black veil was delayed two years, because the Bishop of Antwerp wished to bestow it upon her himself, and he was obliged ' by many weighty affairs to postpone the ceremony.' However, on May 26th, 1791, Bishop Netis went to Lierre, and not only gave the black veil to Sister Mary Aloysia, but also received the vows of three novices, Francis Xaveria Jessop, Mary Teresa Antonia Van Cannart, and Mary Joseph of the Infant Jesus (Broers). The first and last of these became Prioresses.

Mother Francis Xaveria's father was Mr. John

Jessop of Sheffield. She had two elder sisters already professed at Hoogstraet, but the nuns at Lierre being just then (1788) in need of new subjects, they made a novena to St. Francis Xavier, in answer to which (so say the Annals) Sarah Jessop asked to be received at Lierre and was consequently given the Saint's name.

After having twice been Prioress (1817–1820; 1823–1827) Mother Francis Xaveria died on March 11th, 1855, ' in the 89th year of her age ; Jubilarian 17 years.'[1] Her death bill adds :

' This dear Mother was the last relic of our Convent at Lier. We felt her loss very much. God grant we may imitate her great virtues that so we may merit to share in her glory and felicity. Amen.'

Mother Mary Joseph (Mary Magdalen Broers) was the daughter of M. Jean Henri Broers of Mechlin and Anna Maria De Brouwer, his wife. Her family were much opposed to her entering ' a convent of foreigners,' but as God called her to be a Carmelite, and all Carmels in Flanders except the English ones had been suppressed, she was received in Lierre on May 25th, 1790, and professed the following year. After filling various offices ' with great skill and cleverness to the great satisfaction of her Superiors,' she was elected Prioress in 1820, holding that office for three years, and was re-elected in 1826.

' In this laborious office she exercised great zeal and charity towards the community, and it

---

[1] Some MSS. give 1790 as date of her profession; but in neither case would she have been a Jubilarian 17 years.

was owing in great measure to her exertions that
we removed to Carmel House.'

The nuns 'were not very comfortable' while
they lived in Cocken Hall, and were in continual
dread that the rent would be raised above their
means. Therefore, after due consideration, Mother
Mary Joseph purchased their present (1936) property, Carmel House, near Darlington, where
'the community safely arrived on the Friday,
29th of October, 1830.'

There, after a lingering and painful illness, Mother
Mary Joseph died on May 3rd, 1833. She had
been succeeded as Prioress on April 28th, 1830 by
Mother Mary Winifred of the Immaculate Conception, Margaret Walmsley of Bilsborrow. Margaret was the only daughter of Mr. Thomas
Walmsley and Margaret Cattral (Catteral?). She
took the habit of Our Lady of Mount Carmel on
December 18th, 1810, aged 19, and was professed
on December 21st, 1811. As a child she had a great
love of prayer and used to spend hours in the garden
'like a little hermit, occupied in pious reading.'
She entered first with the Benedictines ' at Hammer-
smith in Middlesex near London' (now at Teign-
mouth), but soon found that her true vocation was
to be a Discalced Carmelite, though 'the good
Dames were very sorry to part with her.'

'At the time when the heavy burden of
Superiority fell upon her, we were removing
from Cocken Hall to Carmel House, where she
put everything into the best order she could,
and as conformable to our Rule as was possible.'

The nuns' faithful friend and chaplain, Father Roby, brought the Blessed Sacrament to Carmel House the day the community assembled there— the feast of St. Bede the Venerable, the only English Doctor of the Church. By degrees additional portions were added to the original house, and a beautiful church was built, dedicated to Our Lady Immaculate. After a long delay conventual enclosure was again erected, and the old, peaceful Carmelite life, inaugurated in Lierre about two hundred years previously, has gone on within the walls of Carmel House ever since.

Father Roby died holily, as he had lived, on November 29th, 1841, ' revered as a saint and loved as a parent ' by every member of the community, and was succeeded in his office of chaplain by Father Joseph, later Canon, Brown. Of both these holy priests the nuns, in their gratitude, wrote obituary notices in order that their memory might ever be held in benediction. To Canon Brown, Carmel House is indebted for their

' blessed enclosure, lovely church, and the privilege of dying before Our Lord in the Blessed Sacrament of Love in the Infirmaries[1] our Father planned and built.'

In 1850 Father Brown went to Rome as companion to Dr. Newsham, President of St. Cuthbert's College, Ushaw. On his way back he visited the former Carmel in Lierre, then being used as a factory. After praying by the tomb of Canon

[1] The Infirmaries look down on the nun's choir, so that invalid or dying Sisters can assist at Mass without having to go downstairs.

Edmund Bedingfeld, he listened to accounts of the English Carmelites related to him by some old Lierrois, who told him that their parents often spoke of 'the holy English Teresians.' Their memory was, at that date, still held in veneration in Lierre, where so many of them still lie awaiting God's final Call.

LAUS DEO ET MARIÆ!

INDEX

S

Scholastica, O.S.B., Mother, 3

Simplicity, Instructions on, 107, 108

Stephen, St., 139

Stewart, O.S.B., Mother Hilda, 3

T

Talacre, 1–4, 16, 17

' Ten Aves,' Devotion of the, 120–122

Teresa, St., 9, 16, 29, 30, 34, 66, 67, 101, 117, 118, 127, 130, 131, 139

Teresa of Jesus Ward, 30, 33, 34, 42, 45

Teresa of Jesus Mary Worsley, 115

Teresa of St. Augustine (Mme Louise de France), 133

Teresa of St. Augustine Foster, 63

U

Ursula of All Saints (Elizabeth Mostyn) professed, 19 ; shares her sister's secrets, 9–10, 29–32 ; sent to Lierre, 32 ; disturbed by devils, 46 ; elected Subprioress, 69 ; offers her life for her sister, 73 ; last interview with Mother Margaret, 75 ; elected Prioress, 86 ; eulogy, 132

Ushaw, St. Cuthbert's College, 143

V

Vaughan, Richard, 39

W

Weymouth, 10, 11

White, S.J., Father Andrew, 31, 85, 125

Winifred's Well, St., 129

Worsley, S.J., Father Thomas, 23

The Mayflower Press, Plymouth. William Brendon & Son, Ltd.